CYCLE
ROAD RACING

TOM NEWMAN

THE CROWOOD PRESS

First published in 2013 by
The Crowood Press Ltd
Ramsbury, Marlborough
Wiltshire SN8 2HR

www.crowood.com

British Library Cataloguing-in-Publication Data
A catalogue record for this book is available from the British Library.

ISBN 978 1 84797 434 1

Illustration credits
Keith Shorten – Westerley Cycling Club for many action shots of racing cyclists.
Garmin UK – for equipment photographs and press release.
Westerley CC – team mates for various contributions.
Woolsey of Acton Cycle Shop – for loan of their equipment and time.
The Bike Shop – North Harrow, London, for supplying many of the equipment
photographs.
Malcolm Edwards – good cycling friend.
Bill Butterworth – inspirational West London veteran racing cyclist.
Robert Lawrence of ICT Connect for help with IT.

Finally and not least, Lesley Newman, wife of over thirty-two years for putting up
with him whilst undertaking this venture.

Typeset by Servis Filmsetting Ltd, Stockport, Cheshire

Printed and bound in India by Replika Press Pvt Ltd

CONTENTS

About the Author

Tom Newman is a professional cycling coach and runs Capital Cycle Coaching (www.capitalcyclecoaching.co.uk).

For over forty years he has toured extensively throughout the UK as far north as Cape Wrath and as far south as Land's End. He has also raced in time trials at all distances up to twelve hours and participated in track racing, being a regular competitor at the now demolished Paddington Track, famous among west London cyclists. He has ridden countless road races and dabbled in cyclo-cross. As a one-off, Tom even ran the London Marathon in a respectable time of just over 3.5 hours.

Tom is a life-long member of the Westerley Cycling Club, based in west London, where he has held many positions including race organizer, secretary, club coach and editor of the club magazine, *Club Record*.

Passionate about coaching, Tom has coached many riders to achieve their ambitions and more for over fifteen years. His qualifications include Association of British Cycling Coaches (ABCC) British Cycling – Club Coach, Level 2 Coach and Level 3 Road and Time Trial Coach.

CHAPTER 1

Equipment and Clothing

The Bicycle

These days, there is an enormous choice of bicycles, but before evaluating what is out there, it's best to have a clear idea of what the bike is going to be used for.

Are you intending to road race with occasional time trials, or are you planning only to ride road races or only time trials? If the latter, are you going to concentrate on short-distance events – 10 miles, 25s and maybe the odd 50 – or will you also include long-distance events? There again, you may want to time trial with the occasional road race thrown in. In this case you could purchase a road race bike and have the option of fitting clip-on tri-bars when you time trial.

Before you make any decisions, it's well worth joining a club or teaming up with like-minded souls and seeing the bikes that are ridden in races. It's no secret that the bikes that are ridden in these events have evolved over time and choices are made based on hard facts and experience, and not necessarily on current fads. Look at magazines such as *Cycling Weekly* and visit topical websites,

Modern road racing bike.

Carbon cycle frame.

for example www.ukcyclesport.com, where there are informed articles on equipment and clothing.

Crucially, of course, you must decide your budget: although the latest carbon dream machine looks very tasty, the £5,000 price tag won't!

We all have to start somewhere, and no doubt mistakes will be made along the line, but to coin a phrase 'you have to be in it to win it'. So bite the bullet, decide on what you want and go for it.

Here is an example to help you with the thought process. A friend of mine achieved superb time trial results on a standard road bike, material steel, with clip-on tri-bars. His typical times, were 10 miles – 21 minutes, 25 miles – 54 minutes, 50 miles – 1 hour 54 minutes, superb sub-4 hour 100-mile rides and over 260 miles in 12 hours. This bike cost less than £1,000, and many riders would bite your hand off to achieve these times.

So phenomenal times can be achieved for less than a grand. This figure of £1,000 seems to crop up regularly when I look at race results, and seems the benchmark for bike purchases in terms of value for money. For this money, you normally get a reasonable frame with decent equipment; if you want to upgrade later with better wheels, for example, you can do so. Of course you can pay a lot more and enjoy the benefits associated with the higher price tag, but you won't necessarily go any faster.

The Frame and Fork

Materials

Carbon This is outstripping all materials for producing road frames – and track frames too, come to that. It used to be expensive but mass production has seen the price come down to affordable levels. Its chief characteristic is that the material lends itself to being moulded into shapes and structures that are impossible in other materials, making aerodynamic shapes easy to achieve. The material is also extremely light, strong, stiff and comfortable to ride. Whether its longevity is on a par with steel, for example, remains to be seen. Still, carbon is undoubtedly the most popular material today and is the natural choice for race frames.

Aluminium cycle frame.

Aluminium Just a short while ago, aluminium was the natural choice of frame materials. It is very responsive and stiff, its harshness of ride, compared to steel frames, possibly making it a bit uncomfortable for long-distance events. With special manufacturing techniques aluminium can be formed into a wide assortment of intricate shapes. Lately frames have been built with carbon-fibre seat stays to aid comfort and stiffness and now it's the norm to have a frame fitted with a carbon fork. Prices are generally lower than carbon but how long this continues remains to be seen.

Steel Steel was the choice of champions and still is a superb material, especially with the latest Reynolds 953 top-end tubing. This material is extremely resilient and has excellent high-impact strength and fatigue resistance. Steel is expensive, however, and requires specialized frame builders who understand this material. A number of years ago steel was the only choice, and though it has gone out of fashion now it still has its devotees – there is a sort of cult following, with many independent builders producing fabulous frames.

Titanium Without a doubt titanium offers ultimate durability, but while it is becoming more affordable, it is still expensive. Titanium is very difficult to process and manipulate into shapes. Like all materials, a good titanium frame is marvellous, but beware of the cheaper grades out there. For example, you may find frames with seamed tubing, where a flat sheet is rolled then welded into a tube. Although the frame will have the correct material grade it will not have the same characteristics as the more expensive extruded material. Like so many things in life, if it sounds too good to be true then it is.

Sizing the frame

Too large a frame will be awkward to adjust. For example, you may not be able to drop the handlebars or saddle low enough, which will compromise control; having the saddle too high may also give future knee problems. Too small a frame will again be difficult to adjust: you may end up with an extended seat post and very long handlebar stem. There are a number of valuable websites giving good advice on this subject, and if you type 'Bicycle frame size guide' into your search engine, a number of useful guides will come up. A good cycling shop specializing in racing frames for both road and time trial competition will also offer good advice, so it's well worth developing a relationship with them.

An important consideration for road racing frames is the bottom bracket height. Many races are now on closed circuits, for example Hog Hill, Hillingdon and Crystal Palace in the London area and plenty more throughout the country. These circuits require you to pedal through corners to keep in contention. Therefore you don't want a bottom bracket height that is so low there is a risk of grounding a pedal half way around the corner, with disastrous consequences. Fortunately most modern road racing frames now sold will have a bottom bracket height in excess of 27cm (10.6in) fitted with standard size cranks of 170mm (6.8in).

Setting the saddle height

Although there is more detailed information on this subject later in this book (see Chapter 3), it's worth spending a bit of time on it here.

Taking inseam measurement.

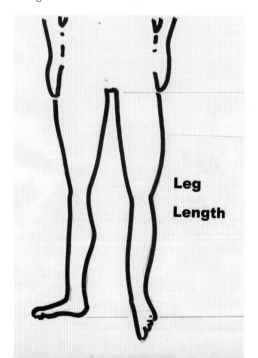

Leg Length

Most information for determining the saddle height is based on one single measurement – the inseam. Standing barefoot on a flat, firm surface against a wall, raise a rigid, straight-edged object, such as a book, between your legs to crotch height. With the aid of a helper, measure from the floor to the point where the top of the book touches your crotch. With this measurement the saddle height can be calculated a couple of ways:

A Multiply your inseam measurement by 0.885. For example, I have an inseam measurement of 79cm (31in); 79cm × 0.885 = 70cm (27.5in) so the saddle height is 70cm above the bottom bracket height. With this measurement there is a slight bend in the knee when the pedal is at its furthest point from the saddle, in line with the seat tube.

B An alternative formula is to multiply the inseam length by 1.09. This calculation will provide a measurement that includes the crank length.

Whilst both of the above formulas will give you a reasonable saddle height measurement, other variables that need to be considered include pedal type, thickness of shoe sole, seat tube angle and personal preference. Thickness of clothing can also be an issue – for example, in the winter, with more layers worn, you may wish to lower the saddle to compensate.

Wheels

Good wheels are crucial, and improving the wheels on your bike is by far one of the best upgrades you can make.

Most popular wheels are built with aluminium rims and small flange hubs, have triple-crossed spokes and use clincher rims. Typically they can be used for all disciplines of cycle sport on the road.

An upgrade will typically be to a lighter wheel. This will take less effort to accelerate

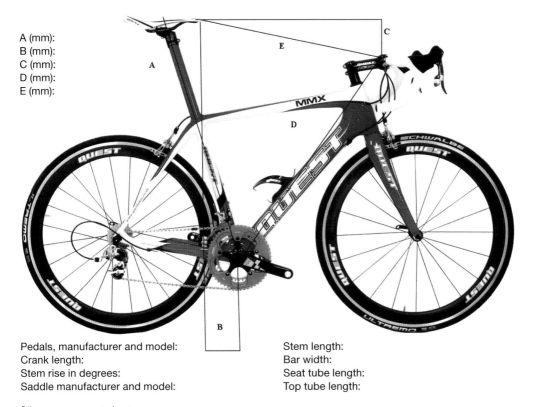

A (mm):
B (mm):
C (mm):
D (mm):
E (mm):

Pedals, manufacturer and model:
Crank length:
Stem rise in degrees:
Saddle manufacturer and model:

Stem length:
Bar width:
Seat tube length:
Top tube length:

Bike measurement chart.

and decelerate, as rotating weight is more significant than static weight. Better-grade wheels also have smoother bearings and will run better and require less maintenance.

On high-end wheel packages carbon is now commonly used. This material can be built into deep section designs, and is extremely rigid and light.

However, an important consideration when selecting wheels is to consider your weight. They must be fit for purpose. Lighter riders can use lighter wheels but a 90kg rider, for example, could easily wreck these in a few short rides so will need a stronger wheel set. You may be better off selecting a good-grade hub, stronger rims and more spokes than the minimal number advertised.

Cross-spoked wheels in a time trial.

Rear disc wheel track option.

Spoking patterns fall broadly into two categories, which have different performance benefits: cross patterns – single-, double- or triple-crossed spokes, and radial patterns, especially for the front wheel – and disc wheels, which have no spokes.

Generally, road racers use spoked wheels of various patterns while time triallers get away with fewer spokes or using disc wheels – which offer less wind resistance so go faster – when appropriate. Hilly courses and windy days will not necessarily suit disc wheels, however, as they are heavier than spoked ones.

Most importantly, with all wheels it is much better to have a lower-cost, well-maintained package than top-end wheels with loose spokes and scored braking surfaces. Don't worry too much about being able to afford top-end wheels for the sake of a few seconds, as many riders have achieved personal bests in time trials using conventional wheels shod with middle-of-the-road tyres.

The kind of terrain being ridden on is another important factor. High-end time trial wheels are fine for time trials, where handling is not such an issue and road surfaces are generally better, while for road racing these two characteristics will certainly come into play.

Most top time triallers in peak season use a carbon-disc rear wheel coupled with a carbon tri-spoke or radial-spoked front wheel, and – if top performance is vital – tubular rims as opposed to clincher rims.

Tubular rims are stronger, being constructed of a box section shod with tubular tyres, with the inner tube sewn inside the outer casing.

Top-end road racing wheels tend to be carbon, but depending on the course and length of race, this material may give too harsh a ride, especially on poorly surfaced roads; aluminium rims may be the better choice for these circumstances. Certainly on closed circuits, top-end wheels tend to be carbon as races are shorter and the road surface is good quality.

Tri-spoked front wheel.

Road racing wheels.

Tyres

Tyres are the only part of the bike in contact with the road so arguably are the most important part. Other than wind resistance, rolling resistance produced by tyres is the largest force acting against forward motion. Try riding a knobbly mountain bike tyre then a slick 23mm-section road tyre on a smooth tarmac road and see for yourself.

There are many factors affecting tyre design, including weight, tread design and material quality. One key decision is whether to use clincher or tubular tyres.

Clincher design has come on immensely over the years and is normally the natural choice for racing cyclists, due to these tyres' affordability and ease of repair. Clincher tyres hook onto the rim bead and must be fitted with a separate inner tube.

Tyre cross-sections showing the amount of kevlar insert in the tread of the tyre.

Tubular tyres (tubs) of comparable quality are more expensive. Tubs can be very lightweight and are completely encased including their own inner tube and must be glued or stuck with strong adhesive tape to the rim surface.

Also, a puncture can often spell the end to the tub, which is a very expensive result, especially if it is being used for the first time. Tubs can be repaired either DIY – and you need to know what you are doing – or sent away for repair. Whichever method you use, the confidence in the product never seems to be the same, however, and the repaired tyre is usually consigned to a spare in case of puncturing in a race. I know this from experience, having repaired many tubs in my time. The complexities of repair are beyond the scope of this book.

With all these negatives you might ask yourself why you would use tubs. The advantages are that you can inflate them to higher pressures, while their suppleness makes them the ultimate racing tyre – especially on good time trial days, when you can experience the roaring noise emitted when flying along a smooth tarmac road. There is a perception that tubs are better quality and that they are less prone to puncture, and if you do suffer a puncture, the latest tyre sealant product seems to work very well in getting you up and running again swiftly.

Whatever choice you make, don't skimp on tyres, as they are one of the biggest factors in racing performance, and don't forget to inflate them to the manufacturer's recommended pressures. For that you need a track pump. Look after your tyres and regularly check for cuts or foreign bodies, such as flints, embedded in the tread; these need to be removed carefully.

Groupsets

This is the name given to the assortment of equipment that includes integrated brake and gear levers, chainset, cassette, and rear and front mechanisms. Three main manufactures – Shimano, Campagnolo and SRAM – dominate the market, although you can purchase individual components by other manufactures, such as excellent British makes, Royce and Hope for example, who both make superb hubs in their range of products.

This is a constantly evolving area of cycle design, and you can now find bikes with seven-, eight-, nine-, ten- and even eleven-speed cassettes; the figures refer to the number of sprockets fitted on the rear cassette. Generally, most modern road and time trial bikes are fitted with ten-speed cassettes from the major manufacturers, but it sometimes seems as though manufacturers are competing with other to insert another sprocket on the cassette every year. Chain wear is a significant factor in this respect, as to fit a cassette with eleven sprockets in a restricted space means that chains have had to become narrower. A thinner chain has less bearing surface compared to a thicker chain, resulting in more wear – that is, the chain wears out more quickly. If you leave it too late before replacing, then both chain and rear cassette will need replacing, which is expensive, so ensure your chain is cleaned regularly and lubricated with good-quality oil. Don't make the common mistake of oiling an already dirty chain as this will only exacerbate wear, with the oil becoming a grinding paste.

All the above-mentioned manufacturers offer superb equipment, especially from their mid-range models upwards, and there is little to choose between them. This is an individual choice for each rider; funnily enough, some riders prefer Campagnolo cassettes because they make a lovely whirring noise when freewheeling.

Riders with smaller hands should look for a model where the reach to the braking/

Chainset.

gear-changing lever is smaller, so they are able to grip more easily.

Chainsets are generally fitted with two rings, inner and outer, for racing. Triple-ring chainsets are more for tourist and sportif riders. Crank length on standard road bikes is normally 170mm–175mm. Chain ring sizes coupled with rear sprocket sizes determine the gear size (see chart, p. 16).

Dual-pivot brakes are by far the most effective kind designed for road bikes. Most mid-range series have a quick-release mechanism, allowing swift removal of wheels. What can change performance is the material used in the brake blocks – a different compound is used on carbon rims compared to alloy rims – which becomes more evident in wet conditions.

Gearing systems

Almost all gearing systems are operated with cables and when correctly adjusted perform very well. Recently launched on the market is Shimano's electronic gear system. Although there are two ranges on the market, with one being less expensive, price will still rule this option out for most people, although changing gear is unbelievably smooth and reliable. Once bikes are fitted with these systems prices will come down, but at the moment only pro teams ride them, which is no bad thing as any gremlins will be ironed out.

Saddle

This is an important area for obvious reasons, as the saddle is the major contact point between you and the bike, excluding handlebars and pedals.

There are differences between male and female pelvic bones. Women have more pronounced ones, and so female riders should only consider women-specific designs, which are generally shorter and wider. This is to accommodate the wide spacing of women's pelvic bones – the ischial tuberosities in particular. Women's saddles tend also to be shorter with a more padded nose section, alleviating pressure on the genitals.

Men's saddles tend to be narrower and thus do not impede leg movement. When choosing a saddle, the main considerations are comfort and weight. Although not entirely proven, there is some evidence suggesting there are more cases of erectile dysfunction

Chainwheel teeth

Sprocket teeth	20	21	22	23	24	25	26	27	28	29	30	31	32	33	34	35	36	37	38	39	40	41	42	43	44	45	46	47	48	49	50	51	52	53	54	55	56	57	58	59	60
9	60	63	66	69	72	75	78	81	84	87	90	93	96	99	102	105	108	111	114	117	120	123	126	129	132	135	138	141	144	147	150	153	156	159	162	165	168	171	174	177	180
10	54	57	59	62	65	68	70	73	76	78	81	84	86	89	92	95	97	100	103	105	108	111	113	116	119	122	124	127	130	132	135	138	140	143	146	149	151	154	157	159	162
11	49	52	54	56	59	61	64	66	69	71	74	76	79	81	83	86	88	91	93	96	98	101	103	106	108	110	113	115	118	120	123	125	128	130	133	135	137	140	142	145	147
12	45	47	50	52	54	56	59	61	63	65	68	70	72	74	77	79	81	83	86	88	90	92	95	97	99	101	104	106	108	110	113	115	117	119	122	124	126	128	131	133	135
13	42	44	46	48	50	52	54	56	58	60	62	64	66	69	71	73	75	77	79	81	83	85	87	89	91	93	96	98	100	102	104	106	108	110	112	114	116	118	120	123	125
14	39	41	42	44	46	48	50	52	54	56	58	60	62	64	66	68	69	71	73	75	77	79	81	83	85	87	89	91	93	95	96	98	100	102	104	106	108	110	112	114	116
15	36	38	40	41	43	45	47	49	50	52	54	56	58	59	61	63	65	67	68	70	72	74	76	77	79	81	83	85	86	88	90	92	94	95	97	99	101	103	104	106	108
16	34	35	37	39	41	42	44	46	47	49	51	52	54	56	57	59	61	62	64	66	68	69	71	73	74	76	78	79	81	83	84	86	88	89	91	93	95	96	98	100	101
17	32	33	35	37	38	40	41	43	44	46	48	49	51	52	54	56	57	59	60	62	64	65	67	68	70	71	73	75	76	78	79	81	83	84	86	87	89	91	92	94	95
18	30	32	33	35	36	38	39	41	42	44	45	47	48	50	51	53	54	56	57	59	60	62	63	65	66	68	69	71	72	74	75	77	78	80	81	83	84	86	87	89	90
19	28	30	31	33	34	36	37	38	40	41	43	44	45	47	48	50	51	53	54	55	57	58	60	61	63	64	65	67	68	70	71	72	74	75	77	78	80	81	82	84	85
20	27	28	30	31	32	34	35	36	38	39	41	42	43	45	46	47	49	50	51	53	54	55	57	58	59	61	62	63	65	66	68	69	70	72	73	74	76	77	78	80	81
21	26	27	28	30	31	32	33	35	36	37	39	40	41	42	44	45	46	48	49	50	51	53	54	55	57	58	59	60	62	63	64	66	67	68	69	71	72	73	75	76	77
22	25	26	27	28	29	31	32	33	34	36	37	38	39	41	42	43	44	45	47	48	49	50	52	53	54	55	56	58	59	60	61	63	64	65	66	68	69	70	71	72	74
23	23	25	26	27	28	29	31	32	33	34	35	36	38	39	40	41	42	43	45	46	47	48	49	50	52	53	54	55	56	58	59	60	61	62	63	65	66	67	68	69	70
24	23	24	25	26	27	28	29	30	32	33	34	35	36	37	38	39	41	42	43	44	45	46	47	48	50	51	52	53	54	55	56	57	59	60	61	62	63	64	65	66	68
25	22	23	24	25	26	27	28	29	30	31	32	33	35	36	37	38	39	40	41	42	43	44	45	46	48	49	50	51	52	53	54	55	56	57	58	59	60	62	63	64	65
26	21	22	23	24	25	26	27	28	29	30	31	32	33	34	35	36	37	38	39	41	42	43	44	45	46	47	48	49	50	51	52	53	54	55	56	57	58	59	60	61	62
27	20	21	22	23	24	25	26	27	28	29	30	31	32	33	34	35	36	37	38	39	40	41	42	43	44	45	46	47	48	49	50	51	52	53	54	55	56	57	58	59	60
28	19	20	21	22	23	24	25	26	27	28	29	30	31	32	33	34	35	36	37	38	39	40	41	41	42	43	44	45	46	47	48	49	50	51	52	53	54	55	56	57	58
29	19	20	20	21	22	23	24	25	26	27	28	29	30	31	32	33	34	34	35	36	37	38	39	40	41	42	43	44	45	46	47	47	48	49	50	51	52	53	54	55	56
30	18	19	20	21	22	23	23	24	25	26	27	28	29	30	31	32	32	33	34	35	36	37	38	39	40	41	41	42	43	44	45	46	47	48	49	50	50	51	52	53	54
31	17	18	19	20	21	22	23	24	24	25	26	27	28	29	30	30	31	32	33	34	35	36	37	37	38	39	40	41	42	43	44	44	45	46	47	48	49	50	51	51	52
32	17	18	19	19	20	21	22	23	24	24	25	26	27	28	29	30	30	31	32	33	34	35	35	36	37	38	39	40	41	41	42	43	44	45	46	46	47	48	49	50	51
33	16	17	18	19	20	20	21	22	23	24	25	25	26	27	28	29	29	30	31	32	33	34	34	35	36	37	38	38	39	40	41	42	43	43	44	45	46	47	47	48	49
34	16	17	17	18	19	20	21	21	22	23	24	25	25	26	27	28	29	29	30	31	32	33	33	34	35	36	37	37	38	39	40	41	41	42	43	44	44	45	46	47	48
35	15	16	17	18	19	19	20	21	22	22	23	24	25	25	26	27	28	29	29	30	31	32	32	33	34	35	35	36	37	38	39	39	40	41	42	42	43	44	45	46	46
36	15	16	17	17	18	19	20	20	21	22	23	23	24	25	26	26	27	28	29	29	30	31	32	32	33	34	35	35	36	37	38	38	39	40	41	41	42	43	44	44	45

Gear table, based on a nominal 27in diameter wheel. The figure quoted (in inches) is the distance the bicycle moves in one complete revolution of the pedals.

Racing saddle.

and impotency problems in male cyclists, which has been linked to reduced blood flow in the pelvic region caused by saddles. To address this, new saddles on the market are designed with a cut-away to reduce the pressure on the internal pudendal arteries.

It is a difficult subject to advise on, with some experienced riders settling on a design/manufacturer they are satisfied with and sticking with this combination throughout their career. But to summarize, lightest is not necessary best and comfort is paramount. For time trials some (not all) riders point their saddles down slightly, but in all other cases it is best to start off with a horizontal position and adjust to suit taste.

Handlebars

Road bike handlebars

Comfort is the most important consideration here. The materials used are aluminium and carbon. All drop handlebars provide the rider with a variety of positions to safely control

Carbon drop handlebars.

One piece tri-bars mounted with end shifters fitted.

the bike. Newer designs include anatomically designed bars, but the traditional bars with drop and reach are still available. The width of the bars should be sufficient not to restrict breathing – a general rule is that they should be shoulder width to achieve this. The drop depth should be enough so that the rider's arms are slightly flexed, not fully extended.

You could consider compact handlebars, with a typical drop of 125mm, if you have small hands or want a higher position. Comfort can be increased by double taping the bars or fitting gel inserts.

With many handlebars now made from carbon, some also include an integral stem to reduce weight compared to the standard design with separate bars and stem. This design is much more expensive, however, and only adjustable in the vertical plane, whereas separates can be adjusted both vertically and horizontally with the use of different-length stems.

Time trial handlebars

This topic is touched on later in this book, but essentially it is vital for riders to minimize their frontal area to reduce frontal drag. Using specific time trial handlebars enables you to achieve this. The materials used are the same as for road bar, with the more expensive carbon bars fitted with both integral tri-bar extensions and stem. However, superb results are achieved every week with clip-on tri-bars fitted to bull-horn handlebars. They are heavier, but not significantly so, especially with clip-on carbon tri-bars. Ideally, when using specific time trial handlebars they should be shod with specific brake and gear levers so the rider can maintain an aerodynamic position when both braking and changing gear.

Again, it is worth checking out equipment used in local time trials to get an idea of what is being used. Just wandering around the car park at an open time trial, maybe taking some snapshots, will help you in making decisions. Have a chat with some of the competitors as well, as most people are only too happy to pass on tips.

Pedals, Cleats and Racing Shoes

A few manufacturers dominate this market and there is really little to choose between them, though of course each manufacturer markets their products as being the best. By and large, on road bike pedals the cleat is fixed to the shoe, projecting from the sole, and slots into the pedal, thus holding your foot tight.

This design revolutionized pedals, compared to the previous toe clip set-up with straps. With the latter, there was some 'float' in the design so knee problems were fairly unusual. With the cleat set-up, by contrast, the foot is sometimes held too rigidly in position with hardly any float, which can lead to knee problems. With cycling being a repetitive action carried out countless times it is essential that the set-up is comfortable to avoid an overuse injury. Maintaining joint flexibility is vital and this is covered in Chapter 5.

Many a cyclist will also have done a tap dance on smooth village halls with this pedal/cleat set-up and ended up as a crumpled heap on the floor looking embarrassed.

There are ways round these issues. Many of my cycling friends used to use Look Delta pedals and fitted them to several bikes. All was fine until this design was phased out and replaced with the Cleo pedal, which had different, incompatible fixing cleats. Some riders took the opportunity to switch to mountain bike pedals. These have double-sided fixing, making it easier to fix your shoe in quickly. Furthermore, the shoes have recessed cleats so the sole of the shoe is flat, making it much easier to walk in. Performance wise, there does not seem to be any noticeable difference and many riders now fit all their bikes

Racing shoes.

with this set-up so they all have the same. This arrangement also gives adequate lateral movement.

Whatever option you choose, pay careful attention to cleat wear. I have seen races lost in the final sprint with riders pulling their foot out from the pedal because of worn cleats not gripping properly.

Comfortable shoes with stiff soles are essential. The stiff sole passes the forces from your muscles through to the pedal. Carbon soles, which are becoming very popular now, are extremely stiff, but some riders find this uncomfortable and prefer something slightly more flexible. With all shoes, the three-point fixing seems to be the favourite system, providing foot security and comfort with the fixing load distributed evenly over the foot.

Fixed Wheel

There are in the UK many devotees of the fixed wheel, where the sprocket is connected rigidly to the hub (no freewheel). Some race this form of bike in time trials; some even train and race on a 'fixed' exclusively, shunning the expensive assortment of accessories on offer. The beauty is the sheer simplicity of the set-up, and with coasting impossible, the connection between rider and machine has an almost Zen-like quality.

Fixed-wheel bikes generally have one gear, direct drive, normally only one front brake and no rear brake. Although you can use a ³⁄₃₂in chain, purists prefer the thicker stronger

Track bike.

Steel-framed fixed wheel time trial bike.

Turbo bike set-up.

⅛in version to withstand both forwards and backwards pedalling forces.

One of the chief virtues is that you can build a bike for far less money than needed for geared versions. Another advantage is that with the minimum of equipment it is very light.

Gearing is the main topic amongst devotees. Generally, 72in is a good all-round gear to ride around on, but the smaller 64in could be more suitable in more hilly areas or where there are lots of stops for road obstructions such as traffic lights.

For racing, anything upwards from 86in is used: maybe 86in on sporting courses, increasing in size to 100in on fast, traffic-assisted courses. There is nothing complicated about it in time trials – you pedal harder into headwinds/on uphill sections and can even pass competitors slogging away overgeared. On the downhill, wind-assisted bits you spin along and try to recover, maybe losing a bit of time to the gear merchants but not as much as you think.

Turbo Trainers

Love them or hate then, for town-based cyclists looking for quality workouts this piece of equipment is essential. I knew one London-based cyclist who never went out on the open road, only training on a turbo and riding on closed circuits, where he took his bike to the circuit in the boot of his car. He achieved good results on this schedule and enjoyed the racing.

Finding a place to mount the turbo with a bike permanently is the key, as it is a chore having to keep setting the bike up. Ideal locations are a shed, garage or even a spare room. In addition have a large clock mounted on the wall with a second hand to time the interval, and a fan to keep you cool. Mount the cycle computer on the rear wheel to monitor speed, and if you have a cadence sensor as well even better. To complete it all, drape a towel over the top tube/headset to catch the salty drips of sweat and take a bottle.

With a bewildering array of options, which one do you choose? Having conducted many turbo sessions at my club and been involved in charity events, I've honed the choice down to two types: magnetic and electronic.

Magnetic turbos usually consist of a couple of rotating magnets, and the resistance felt when cycling is caused by the force that is created by the two magnets being attracted towards each other. The resistance is adjusted remotely by either changing a handlebar lever or on the trainer itself. Generally, the more you pay for them, the quieter they are and more robust the construction, which is essential as they receive a good battering.

If you mount your computer on the rear wheel, you can gain many of the functions that come with the more expensive electronic range. For example, I use a system made by Garmin and mount the sensor in this fashion coupled with a cadence sensor, and I use my heart monitor as well. With this range of accessories and the readings on the Garmin, such as speed, average speed and distance, there is whole host of data to look at.

Electronic turbos are the most expensive. Many of these can display a whole host of information, such as heart rate (when you have a HR chest strap fitted), power in watts, distance covered and average speed. The more expensive type can be linked to a computer and you can ride a simulated race, hillclimb or whatever competition you upload into the computer – in effect, virtual racing. In my cycling club we use electronic turbos at our club room and calibrate them accurately so all riders are using the same resistance and we can hold simulated races to get us through the winter months.

Modern turbo trainer models coming on the market now have a unique, natural side-to-side motion. With this lateral motion core muscles are engaged to maintain balance so you simulate out-of-the-saddle hillclimb intervals.

This is the kind of equipment that is continually evolving, so keeping up to date requires regularly looking to see what is out there.

Clothing

With the wide, competitively priced range of clothing available on the market today, cyclists have never had it so good. Ensure whatever you wear fits snugly but not too tightly.

Summer Cycling

Helmet Helmets are compulsory for all UK road races but really should be worn at all times when out on the road. So many good makes are available; choose one that conforms to a recognized standard. Key points are ventilation, weight and aerodynamics (especially for time trials). As helmets go up in price, they generally offer greater ventilation and lighter

Cycling helmet – the most expensive doesn't necessarily mean the best, but they provide better head fixing and more air vents, and they are lighter.

weight, and invariably better adjustment and comfort.

Time trial helmets are intended to be aerodynamic and therefore have no vents. The popular teardrop helmets are designed so that when the rider's head is correctly positioned, the tail is flush with the back. Moving out of this position negates the aerodynamic benefits. Interestingly, the winning rider in the 2011 British time trial championships wore a shorter helmet fitted with a visor.

Short-sleeved race jersey Choose a jersey with rear pockets. Some now come with a full-length zip, making it easier to put on and adjust for varying weather conditions.

Long-sleeved jersey Although not essential, these are very handy for cooler weather.

Undervest Many vests now are made from material that wicks sweat away from your body. Whatever the conditions, an undervest is desirable in the UK. In the summer,

if you crash wearing only a lycra top with no undervest, road rash to your body is likely, as the lycra is easily punctured and the material 'sticks' to the road. Your flesh will slide over the garment thus causing skin-burn or road rash. If you wear an undervest, this rather than your skin will slide over the lycra, thus protecting you.

Arm and leg warmers These are easy to put on and remove when conditions warm up, and are also handy for warming up in.

Shorts Good-quality bib shorts are a cyclist's godsend. Buy the best you can afford: when riding long distances the comfort you experience is worth every penny. Look after them well, washing them after every ride for hygienic reasons. As with most modern synthetics, they can be machine washed and dry quickly. Aim to have two or three pairs.

Mitts These should be ridden with all the time. The padding in the gel inserts largely eliminates road vibration, and if you are involved in a crash they protect your hands from road rash. Don't forget to wash them regularly for hygienic reasons; many cyclists wipe their face with them during races, which can spread bacteria.

Skinsuit A skinsuit is one of the most aerodynamic pieces of clothing you will ever purchase. These are normally worn in time trials or circuit races, which are shorter in duration than road races. Skinsuits are much better than separate shorts and vests, and many now come with pockets neatly sewn in to carry your valuables. Ensure that it is tight fitting.

Socks Don't skimp on quality with socks. Most are now made from Coolmax, a wonderful material for temperature control. It used to be de rigueur for road cyclist to wear white ones that were cut just above the ankle; black was frowned upon. Latest

Cycling skinsuit – if there is one piece of clothing or equipment that will improve your performance, then this is it.

Winter Cycling

All of the above except skinsuits are worn, but add the following to keep out the winter chills:

Winter jacket A good jacket makes cycling so much more pleasurable on bitter cold days and becomes your best friend. Buy the best you can afford as this garment comes in for a lot of abuse. Choose one with lots of reflective material – you want to be seen.

Bib tights Wear these over your racing shorts. Some now come with padded inserts but this is not essential, especially with racing shorts underneath.

Long-sleeved undervest This can be made out of similar material to the summer vest. Wear your racing vest over the top to provide pockets to store your valuables whilst out on a training ride.

Long-sleeved jersey It is much better to have several layers of thin clothing to keep warm rather than one thick one, as air is trapped between the layers. If you get too hot you can always remove a layer.

Racing cape or waterproof jacket One of the best purchases I ever made was a rain jacket made out of Gore-Tex. Although very expensive, it's a godsend on wet or raw, cold days as it is worn over the top of everything.

Gloves There is nothing so miserable as suffering with cold hands on a ride. Many makes now advertise what temperatures they can be ridden in. Top-quality gloves invariably come with velcro fixing and long cuffs so you can tuck your jacket sleeves inside, thus keeping all extremities well covered up. Cycling-specific gloves are padded in the important places, such as the index finger and thumb, which experiences maximum wear as this part grips the brake hood.

fashions dictate any colour goes, however, and lengths go up to mid-calf with some well-known British professionals. Bear in mind that in the British climate long socks can quickly turn into a soggy mess.

Eyewear Glasses provide protection from both UV rays and grit thrown up from the road. Better-quality glasses come with straight ear pieces so they can be placed into your helmet slots when not required whilst out riding.

Socks Materials such as merino wool offer great insulation and are hard-wearing. Fashion is not so important as with summer socks.

Shoes It is best to have a separate pair of shoes for the winter, a pair that is more robust, thicker and thus warmer.

Overshoes These are essential for eliminating cold feet. They keep your feet dry and protect those valuable shoes from damp, mucky roads.

Hat I always advocate wearing a helmet, and to keep your head and ears warm there are many thin hats that fit underneath. In less cold conditions wear a racing cap underneath the helmet. The peak is useful when riding into low-lying sun as it gives eye protection.

Eyewear Exchange tinted for clear glasses in the winter.

Mudguards Not a piece of clothing, but this piece of equipment protects both your bike and you from road spray – witness the black skid mark up riders' backs. Many race bikes don't have eyelets to clamp standard mudguards to the frame, but there are now carbon mudguards on the market that come with their own fixings and provide excellent protection. They don't rattle when riding if fitted properly.

CHAPTER 2

Training

In my youth I once read an old cycling book called *The Complete Cyclist* by Harold Moore (one of my favourite cycling books of all time). One of the chapters concentrated on Training for Cycle Races. I quote:

> As the racing season opens just before Easter, training spins should begin in March, say two evening rides of about twenty miles each week. A low gear of 65 inches should be used during these introductory rides, which should be followed, where possible, by a warm bath or brisk rub down, a drink of hot milk or a good liquid food, according to taste.
>
> This, coupled with the weekend mileage, was deemed sufficient, as you didn't want to wear yourself out!

If it really was this simple we could all achieve our goals. But it never is, as work, meetings, family time and lots of other events always seem to intervene to derail our plans.

The general principles still apply, however, and a key one is consistency. It is most important to make your training specific: for example, there is no need to ride long miles at Z2 intensity (see opposite) if you are only going to compete in 10-mile time trials. On the other hand, there is no point solely riding short, sharp, high-intensity turbo sessions if you are only going to compete in a 12-hour event. You have to decide what is needed to ride a 23-minute 10-mile time trial and train accordingly.

Devising a Training Programme

Before you embark on your training programme, ask yourself the following questions:

What do I want to achieve and by when?
You could be on a mission to break the hour for 25 miles or finish in a fourth category road race in two years' time. No matter what the objective or how far off it is, have a goal and commit, as in my experience this focuses the mind and brings the greatest results.

How much time can I devote to it?
This should be calculated in hours not miles. For example, a tough mountain bike over undulating terrain for an hour is a pretty tough ride compared to a two-hour road ride on smooth, tarmac, mainly flat roads, with hardly any effort exerted. So your hour on the turbo fitted into a lunchtime session could be very tough and rewarding. Try to match your training with the type of races you are riding.

I once carried out a survey on many club racing cyclists to find out approximately how many hours they trained a week, and it worked out at six to eight hours. If you are also working full time this is a big commitment in time, so make it work. The funny thing was the difference in results. Some riders achieved first category road racing status and others broke the hour and two hours for 25- and 50-mile time trials respectively, while other riders plodded along achieving the same sorts of results they had for many years. It simply comes down to quality not quantity – as stated above, training should be event-specific.

Breaking up this training time crudely, it works out to two or three hour-long sessions per week coupled with a longer three- to four-hour weekend ride. For cyclists with partners or families, domestic bliss can be normally maintained with this volume. So I will use this pattern as the basis for this chapter, as I've found out with experience that it works well. Of course, if you do have more time available then make it work for you.

Where can I train? A cyclist holed up in central London is going to find it difficult to get out on the open road to ride specific intervals, given the obvious dangers such as traffic. The turbo is the recognized tool to fill the gap. Armed with a turbo and the weekend ride there are countless sessions that can be ridden, so there is no excuse for falling short. Many cyclists commute by bike, so with creative planning this can be incorporated into the training programme to give the desired intensity.

Before going into more detail it is best to have an understanding of the different training zones for cyclists devised by British Cycling (BC) in the mid-1980s by cycling sports scientist Peter Keen. Originally developed with four zones it was later expanded to five levels with one extra added, the recovery zone. The French and US national cycling organizations differ, using eight and five zones, respectively; which is better is a matter of personal preference. For this book I am using BC's zones which are given in the 'Zone Training' table.

VO$_2$max is the maximum capacity at which someone can transport and use oxygen during incremental exercise.

Lactate threshold, sometimes called the anaerobic threshold, it is the point when the intensity of effort results in an abrupt increase of blood lactate concentration. Continued exercise beyond this point results in rapid muscle fatigue.

Zone Training

	Training Zone	% MHR	%VO$_2$ max	Blood Lactate mm	RPE (rate of perceived exertion)	Duration of a continuous training session
	Recovery	<60	<42	<1	1 – very light	<1 hour
Basic	Zone 1	60–65	42–49	35–45	2 – light	1.5–6 hours
Basic	Zone 2	65–75	49–63	1.5–2.0	3 – moderate	1–4 hours
Intensive	Zone 3	75—82	63–72	2.0–2.5	5 – heavy	45 mins–3 hours
Intensive	Zone 4	82–89	72–83	2.5–3.5	6	30 mins–1 hour
Maximal	Zone 5	89–94	83–92	3.5–6.0	7 – very heavy	15–40 mins
Maximal	Zone 6	94+	92–100	>6.0	10 – extremely heavy	Intervals

Description of Zones

Z1	Very easy	Recovery zone, steady walking pace
Z2	Easy	Chatting freely
Z3	Steady	Chatting takes an effort
Z4	Brisk	More than a short sentence is impossible
Z5	Hard	You're breathing too hard for more than the odd word
Z6	Very hard	Grunt! Gasp! Pant!

RPE (rate of perceived exertion), commonly known as the Borg scale, is a scale used to indicate a quantitative feeling of fatigue, with 1 being the lowest and 10 being maximum exertion.

The training I prescribe is based on heart rate – HR. The latest methods are based on power. For this you will need to invest in appropriate equipment, such as power cranks, hubs or the latest piece of equipment – the pedal-based power meter. Rate of perceived exertion (RPE) is another tool that is used by many riders. Undoubtedly each method has its merits, with RPE probably being more effective for the experienced rider who knows their body better.

There is no doubt that power expressed in watts is a much more accurate tool than HR, and its use for elite cyclists is vital. For example, power comparisons can be made across the board for various types of cyclists. An elite rider's peak muscle power is 1,600W compared to 1,000W for a 4th-category rider, so you can immediately see that in order to attain elite status you need to be able to exert this amount of power regardless of what heart rate you are showing. The drawbacks are that the equipment is expensive, it has to be calibrated accurately and cannot be easily transported from one bike to another – and it's another gadget on the handlebars.

I have read articles questioning senior coaches on their methods – whether they use HR or power, and which is best. The response is mixed, so one conclusion you can draw is that no single method is best. If you are a rider that likes facts and figures, graphs and accurate data then power is probably for you, especially when using appropriate software such as WKO.

The sheer simplicity of HR is its chief advantage, and it can easily be correlated to speed: for example, if on your turbo at 20mph your HR is 155bpm, this gives you a benchmark every time you exercise on the same turbo set-up (that means with the same tyre, tyre pressure and turbo resistance).

You can make training as technical as you like, and many riders certainly do. But the overriding fact is that you simply have to get out and train and there are no short cuts. Consistency and hard work are key. You can have every conceivable gadget that has ever been invented but without these two qualities you will not hit your goals.

So, no excuses: identify your goals and train for them.

The Components of Fitness

Component	Description	Type of race
Aerobic endurance (AE)	The ability to ride for a long period at a low level	Used in all cycling events that are longer than two minutes (all the ones in this book)
Flexibility (Flex)	The ability to carry out a range of movements around a joint or joints, for example knee and back	Necessary in time trials to hold an aerodynamic position. Being flexible can reduce injury in the event of a crash
Muscle Power (MP)	The ability to produce a high power output over a short period of time	Essential for sprinting in road races
Short-term muscular endurance (STME)	The ability to be able to sustain a high power output for a limited period	Used in attacks in road races
Speed (SP)	The ability to change cadence quickly and achieve a high cadence	Ideal for riders of fixed wheel bikes in time trials
Strength (Str)	The ability of muscles or groups of muscles to generate a maximum amount of force against a resistance	Mainly for sprint riders in track events, but interestingly endurance riders also tend to be stronger than sedentary persons of a similar size

Components of Fitness

Another aspect to get your mind around is the components of fitness for cyclists, the building blocks, so to speak. Fitness is not just fitness – there are different types of fitness and different events demand different levels of those types. You will see, for example, that time trial riders will focus mainly on AE, flexibility and SP, while road race riders focus on all aspects.

The Training Programme

Normally the training calendar is split into four periods of time: preparation, pre-competition, competition and, finally, recovery. There is no hard and fast rule about starting your training on 1 January but the turn of the year seems to kindle cycling spirits and training often kicks off then. If the weather is bad and restricts your getting out, then certainly push the training back.

Unlike many books that specify exact number of miles, hours and precise days to ride, working in the real world I find it better to advise on generalities and let riders work this into their individual calendars.

For each type of rider the components of fitness that need to be worked into the training schedule are outlined below with the most important being listed first and every other rated slightly less accordingly.

Time Trial Rider

Preparation This phase will focus on AE, STME and flexibility and generally lasts for about eight to twelve weeks, thus taking the rider into March. Although racing can be commenced in March, accept performances

Time trial rider shown in early morning TT.

will be compromised so early in the programme. You may not want to race on your best bike.

Pre-Comp This phase will focus on AE, SP, STME, MP and tactical riding, and generally lasts for about six weeks, thus taking the rider into April, when the clocks go forward and evenings become lighter.

Competition Focus on STME, AE, SP. This period of time for most racing cyclists is normally too long and can last from April until October. If you are intending to race this late into the year, it's probably best to have a mid-season break for recovery, followed by a two- to four-week pre-comp phase before starting competition again. Alternatively, limit your competition phase to a maximum of twelve weeks.

Recovery After the season finishes have a period of two weeks off the bike, or if you do ride then keep it really low level. Start back with rest and active recovery,

flexibility building up to AE rides and Str in the gym.

Road Race Rider

The same four training phases apply as for the time trialler, but the emphasis is on different fitness components.

Preparation focuses on AE, Str and SP.

Pre-Comp Tactical, STME, MP and AE training.

Competition STME, MP, SP and tactical.

Recovery Active recovery and rest, technical followed by AE, Str.

You can see that tactics play a far more important part in training here, as in road racing the strongest rider doesn't always win and the more tactically astute rider can have the edge.

Training is not just about simply riding the bike. You have to consider psychological and technical factors as well as concentrating on a good nutritional strategy, so you are prepared

Road race rider on the attack flat out.

Typical circuit road race league starting off.

for competition in every way. A top pro once said that cycling is 80 per cent in your head and the rest is your legs; he was suggesting that having a good head and suspect legs was better than having good legs and unsound head.

So now you know what components of fitness you have to focus on you can work out how to fit these into your training plan. As with most things, if you come up with a way that is simple, easy to understand and to implement then you are more likely to stick to it.

Cyclist Matt Seaton wrote an autobiographical account of being a bike racer and how it intertwined with his own personal life, called *The Escape Artist* (2002). Training in the summer was simple – a criterium at Crystal Palace on Tuesday evening followed by training on Thursday, and road race on Sunday with maybe a shorter Saturday event plus the short commuting ride. Matt was a fine 1st-category rider though he never hit big highs – or lows.

The point is that he worked his training into his working week so it became a natural thing to do and it was simple to effect. Most of us can probably devote two sessions per week, possibly three, and a weekend ride, if we are totally honest with ourselves. Making the best use of this time is the key. I have found that I get my inspiration from reading articles by cyclists who achieve excellent results and reveal how they train.

7-hour road race plan

Week	Monday	Tuesday	Wednesday	
1	Rest day or easy commute to work	Evening race or 90min P1, with 10 x 15sec sprints seated, 5min recovery between each block	Rest day or easy commute to work	
2	Rest day or easy commute to work	Evening race or 90min P1, with 10 x 15sec sprints seated, 5min recovery between each block	Rest day or easy commute to work	
3	Rest day or easy commute to work	Evening race or 90min P1, with 10 x 15sec sprints seated, 5min recovery between each block	Rest day or easy commute to work	
4	Rest day or easy commute to work	Evening race or 90min P1, with 10 x 15sec sprints seated, 5min recovery between each block	Rest day or easy commute to work	
5	Rest day or easy commute to work	Evening race or 90min M2 Z4/5 – 10min Z1 then Z2, including 2 x 15min Z4, with 5min recovery between each block	Rest day or easy commute to work	

Putting It All Together

Before intensive training starts, you have to build a base of endurance miles. These should be ridden at Z2/lower-level Z3; if going up hills you will hit higher zones but don't be too concerned about this. The purpose of getting a good base in is to support you when training changes to more, higher-intensity intervals. Without this endurance base you will not be able to support this training and will simply break down. An accepted standard is that by Easter a good base to have accumulated is about 1,500–2,000 miles. If these are ridden at an average speed of 15mph, the lower figure of 1,500 miles is 100 hours. Divide this figure by, say, fourteen weeks gives you 7 hours per week riding, more if you can manage it. So that you are ready to race, in March some interval training can be introduced.

Twelve-Week Road Race Training Plan

Below is a typical twelve-week schedule for a road race rider training 7 hours a week throughout the season.

Codes beginning with Z refer to the intensity of effort, as per the chart on p. 28, so for instance Z2 is light intensity.

Codes beginning with M, P, E or T refer to the type of workout and these are explained in more detail in Chapter 6. E refees to endurance workouts, M to muscular endurance, P to power and T to time trial test.

Thursday	Friday	Saturday	Sunday
60min M2 Z3 with 8 × 5sec sprints seated, 5min recovery between each block	Rest day or easy commute to work	Race or 90min M2 Z4/5 with 5 × 30sec intervals seated, 30sec recovery after each block	Race as Saturday or 2–3hr E3/P1 to include 10 × 8sec sprints
60min M2 Z3 with 8 × 5 sec sprints seated, 5min recovery between each block	Rest day or easy commute to work	Race or 90min M2 Z4/5 to include 2 × 5min blocks with 30sec Z5, 30sec recovery, 5min recovery between blocks	Race as Saturday or 2–3hr E3/P1 to include 10 × 8sec sprints
60min M2 Z3 with 8 × 5sec sprints seated, 5min recovery between each block	Rest day or easy commute to work	Race or 90min M2 Z4/5 with 3 blocks of 5min alternating 30sec Z5 with 30sec recovery, with 5min recovery between blocks	Race as Saturday or 2–3hr E3 P1 to include 10 × 8sec sprints
25min or 10-mile T2 turbo test. Record average speed, HR, power (if available)	Rest day or easy commute to work	Race or 90min M2 Z3 to include 10 × 15sec seated sprints with 5min recovery between each block	E2 2–3hr – just to enjoy
60min – 15min M2 Z4 then 7min Z4, 5min Z4, 3min Z4 with 1min recovery between each block	Rest day or easy commute to work	Race or 90min M2 Z3 to include 3 blocks of 5min alternating 30sec Z5, 30sec recovery, with 5min recovery between blocks	Race as Saturday or 3hr 15min E2/M2 Z4/5 to include 20min Z4, 15min Z4, 10min Z4 with 5min recovery between each block

continued overleaf

Week	Monday	Tuesday	Wednesday	
6	Rest day or easy commute to work	Evening race or 90min – 10min M2 Z4/5 including 20min Z4 and 10min Z4 with 5min recovery between each block	Rest day or easy commute to work	
7	Rest day or easy commute to work	Evening race or 90min M2 Z4/5 but include 30min Z4 during the last 30min	Rest day or easy commute to work	
8	Rest day	90min Z1/Z2	Rest day	
9	Rest day or easy commute to work	Evening race or 90min P1, with 10 x 15sec sprints seated, 5min recovery between each block	Rest day or easy commute to work	
10	Rest day or easy commute to work	90min – 10min M2 Z4/5 then include 30min Z4 in last hour	Rest day or easy commute to work	
11	Rest day or easy commute to work	90min M2 Z4/5 – include 30min Z4 in last hour	Rest day or easy commute to work	
12	Week of rest			

This is a generalized plan so you can see there is no mention of specific disciplines such as climbing or sprinting, so these will have to be worked in specially. For example, if hill climbing is a weakness that needs to be improved there are many sessions that can be ridden to improve this aspect. You may have an individual goal to climb a training hill beating your best time, thus giving you confidence. See the Special Disciplines section later in this chapter for tips on how to improve them.

One important aspect is regular testing that can be repeated. This may be on a turbo trainer or a measured stretch of road ridden out and back to cancel out wind effect. The most important aspect is that it can be repeated with the same parameters so you can accurately gauge your progress.

Thursday	Friday	Saturday	Sunday
60min – 15min M2 Z4 including 2 × 10min Z4 with 5min recovery between each block	Rest day or easy commute to work	Race or 90min M2 Z3 to include 3 blocks of 5min alternating 30sec Z5, 30sec recovery, with 5min recovery between blocks	Race as Saturday or 3hr 15 min E2/M2 Z4/5 to include 20min Z4, 15min Z4, 10min Z4 with 5min recovery between each block
60min – 15min M2 Z4/5, 9min Z4, 7min Z4, 5min Z4, 3min Z4, 1min recovery between each block	Rest day or easy commute to work	Race or 90min Z2 to include 3 blocks of 5min alternating 30sec Z5, 30sec recovery, with 5min recovery between blocks	Race as Saturday or 3hr E2/M2 Z4/5 to include 25min Z4, 20min Z4, 15min Z4, with 5min recovery between each block
25min or 10-mile T2 turbo test. Record average speed, HR, power (if available)	Rest day	Race or 90min E2	E2 3hr – just for enjoyment
60min M2 Z3 with 8 × 5sec sprints seated, 5min recovery between each block	Rest day or easy commute to work	Race or 90min M2 Z4/5 but include 2 blocks of 7min alternating 30sec Z5, 30sec recovery, with 5min recovery between blocks	Race as Saturday or 3hr E2/M2 Z4/5 to include 25min Z4, 20min Z4, 15min Z4, with 5min recovery between each block
60min M2 Z4/5 with 10min, 8min, 6min Z4, with 1min recovery between each block	Rest day or easy commute to work	Race or 90min M2 Z4/5 to include 2 blocks of 8min alternating 30sec Z5 with 30sec recovery, with 5min recovery between blocks	Race as Saturday or 3hr E2/M2 Z4/5 to include 2 × 30min Z4 with 10min recovery between
60min M2 Z4/5 with 7min, 5min, 3min, 1min Z4, with 1min recovery between each block	Rest day or easy commute to work	Race or 90min M2 Z4/5 to include 4 blocks of 5min alternating 30sec Z5 with 30sec recovery, with 5min recovery between blocks	Race as Saturday or 3hr E2/M2 Z4/5 to include 40min Z4, 20min Z4, 20min Z4, with 5–10min recovery between blocks

Twelve-Week Time Trial Race Training Plan

This programme is mainly intended for short-distance time trials of 10 and 25 miles. For longer distances weekend rides will become longer. A good way of increasing mileage whilst racing is to ride out to local events, race and then ride home.

The longer interval sessions for the time trial programme can be ridden on both road and turbo. The main thrust of the programme is speed, simply speed. Of course the intervals can be adjusted, as they will not necessarily suit everyone. Chapter 6 focuses on turbo-ridden interval sessions.

Regarding zones, there is a consensus that spending too much time in Zone 4, especially for road race riders, is best avoided as it may cause staleness; this level of intensity has been labelled, maybe unfairly, as a no man's land, as you are working too hard to build aerobic fitness but not hard enough to build short-term sprint power. This may hold true for road race riders, who have to cope with sudden changes of pace and terrain, but for time trial riders Zone 4 is very rewarding.

7-hour time trial race plan

Week	Monday	Tuesday	Wednesday	
1	Rest day or easy commute to work	Evening race or 60min to include 10–15min warm-up then 3 x 3min Z5 with 2min recovery between blocks	60min Z2 with 2 x 15sec sprints after warm-up and 10min before session end	
2	Rest day or easy commute to work	Evening race or 60min to include 10–15min warm-up then 4 x 3min Z5 with 2min recovery between blocks	60min Z2 with 2 x 15sec sprints after warm-up and 10min before session end	
3	Rest day or easy commute to work	Evening race or 60min to include 10–15min warm-up then 5 x 3min Z5 with 2min recovery between blocks	60min Z2 with 2 x 15sec sprints after warm-up and 10min before session end	
4	Rest day or easy commute to work	Evening race or 60min to include 10–15min warm-up then 6 x 3min Z5 with 2min recovery between blocks	Rest day or easy commute to work	
5	Rest day or easy commute to work	Evening race or 60min Z2 with 2 x 15sec sprints evenly spread	Rest day or easy commute to work	
6	Rest day or easy commute to work	Evening race or 60min to include 10–15min warm-up then 3 x 3min Z5 with 2min recovery between blocks	Rest day or easy commute to work	
7	Rest day or easy commute to work	Evening race or 60min to include 10–15min warm-up then 4 x 3min Z5 with 2min recovery between blocks	Rest day or easy commute to work	
8	Rest day or easy commute to work	Evening race or 60min to include 10–15min warm-up then 5 x 3min Z5 with 2min recovery between blocks	Rest day or easy commute to work	
9	Rest day or easy commute to work	Evening race or 60min to include 10–15min warm-up then 6 x 3min Z5 with 2min recovery between blocks	Rest day or easy commute to work	
10	Rest day or easy commute to work	Evening race or 60min Z2 with 2 x 15sec sprints evenly spread	Rest day or easy commute to work	

Thursday	Friday	Saturday	Sunday
60min to include 10–15min warm-up then 4 x 30sec Z6 with 3min recovery between blocks	Rest day or easy commute to work	Race or 60min Z2 with 2 x 15sec sprints seated, with 20min between each	Race or 3hr Z2 with 2 x 15sec sprints evenly spread in the ride
60min to include 10–15min warm-up then 6 x 30sec Z6 with 3min recovery between blocks	Rest day or easy commute to work	Race or 60min Z2 with 2 x 15sec sprints seated, with 20min between each block	Race or 3hr Z2 with 2 x 15sec sprints evenly spread in the ride
60min to include 10–15min warm-up then 8 x 30sec Z6 with 3min recovery between blocks	Rest day or easy commute to work	Race or 60min Z2 with 2 x 15sec sprints seated, with 20min between each block	Race or 3hr Z2 with 2 x 15sec sprints evenly spread in the ride
60min to include 10–15min warm-up then 10 x 30sec Z6 with 3min recovery between blocks	Rest day or easy commute to work	Race or 60min Z2 with 2 x 15sec sprints seated, with 20min between each block	Race or 3hr Z2 with 2 x 15sec sprints evenly spread in the ride
60min to include 15min Z2 then 4 x 10sec flat-out sprint with 2min recovery between each block	Rest day or easy commute to work	Race or 60min Z2 with 2 x 15sec sprints seated, with 20min between each block	Race or 3hr Z2 with 2 x 15sec sprints evenly spread in the ride
60min to include 15min Z2 then 2 x 1min Z5 with 1min recovery between each block	Rest day or easy commute to work	Race or 60min Z2 with 2 x 15sec sprints seated, with 20min between each block	Race or 3hr Z2 with 2 x 15sec sprints evenly spread in the ride
60min to include 10–15min warm-up then 4 x 30sec Z6 with 3min recovery between blocks	Rest day or easy commute to work	Race or 60min Z2 with 2 x 15sec sprints seated, with 20min between each block	Race or 3hr Z2 with 2 x 15sec sprints evenly spread in the ride
60min to include 10–15min warm-up then 6 x 30sec Z6 with 3min recovery between blocks	Rest day or easy commute to work	Race or 60min Z2 with 2 x 15sec sprints seated, with 20min between each block	Race or 3hr Z2 with 2 x 15sec sprints evenly spread in the ride
60min to include 10–15min warm-up then 8 x 30sec Z6 with 3min recovery between blocks	Rest day or easy commute to work	Race or 60min Z2 with 2 x 15sec sprints seated, with 20min between each block	Race or 3hr Z2 with 2 x 15sec sprints evenly spread in the ride
60min to include 15min Z2 then 4 x 10sec flat-out sprint with 2min recovery between each block	Rest day or easy commute to work	Race or 60min Z2 with 2 x 15sec sprints seated, with 20min between each block	Race or 3hr Z2 with 2 x 15sec sprints evenly spread in the ride

continued overleaf

37

Week	Monday	Tuesday	Wednesday	
11	Rest day or easy commute to work	Evening race or 60min to include 10–15min warm-up then 3 x 3min Z5 with 2min recovery between blocks	Rest day or easy commute to work	
12	Rest day or easy commute to work	Evening race or 60min to include 10–15min warm-up then 4 x 3min Z5 with 2min recovery between blocks	Rest day or easy commute to work	

Old-School Training

Touched on earlier in this chapter was the importance of getting the miles in pre-season. I'll give an example. My friend Malcolm Edwards was a more than capable time trialler, achieving 10 miles in 20 minutes, 25 miles in 53 minutes, 50 miles in 1 hour 53 minutes, 100 miles in 3 hours 51 minutes and 264 miles in 12 hours.

His training programme consisted of getting in over 2,000 miles between 1 January and Easter. In March he would ride 200k audax events every weekend, which are hard and very strenuous. He wouldn't hang around either: most sessions were ridden at over 17mph, uphill and downhill. Many people think the terrain in north London is flat, but try riding in the Chiltern Hills at this speed and you will be surprised how hilly it is.

Malcolm in his retirement from racing looking relaxed and content.

Thursday	Friday	Saturday	Sunday
60min to include 10–15min warm-up then 8 x 30sec Z6 with 3min recovery between blocks	Rest day or easy commute to work	Race or 60min Z2 with 2 x 15sec sprints seated, with 20min between each block	Race or 3hr Z2 with 2 x 15sec sprints evenly spread in the ride
60min to include 15min Z2 then 2 x 1min Z5 with 1min recovery between each block	Rest day or easy commute to work	Race or 60min Z2 with 2 x 15sec sprints seated, with 20min between each block	Race or 3hr Z2 with 2 x 15sec sprints evenly spread in the ride

The first race on the calendar was Good Friday, and after that he would ride two mid-week events – a 10-mile time trial on Tuesday and a 15-mile one on Thursday, which he would ride out to and back – with a short recovery ride on Saturday and a Sunday race. Starting off with 25-mile races, he would gradually build up the distances. Sometimes he may have ridden two events in one weekend, but this would be the exception and not the rule. When he rode 12-hour events, the mileage would be upped in June, with an odd 300k audax event (long-distance ride with a time limit).

He did not use interval training but relied on racing to build the speed, and never used the turbo but was always out on the road. It worked for Malcolm and no doubt will work for many others, but not for all.

If every coach simplistically prescribed this sort of training without looking closely at personal circumstances, the potentially fine achievements by riders who can't devote this amount of time would not be realized. I can testify to the many riders who live in the London area who exclusively turbo train during the week, only taking to the roads at weekends, but still achieve fine results, especially in short distance events and closed road circuit events.

A good aerobic base underpins everything and this can be achieved by consistency. Don't ignore short rides that add up, like the trip to the shops. Use the bike where you can – and that can be the folding bike with 'civvies' on. Every bit counts.

Keep a training diary, whether it's computerized or plain old paper. It is a good reference tool to look back on. A spreadsheet design is shown on p. 40 that uses different colours for various activities and zones. Many computer aids can now host web-based diaries so your coach can see them first hand (see Chapter 7).

Understanding Training Terms

Keeping things simple is the key, but it is worth knowing the training jargon so you have some idea of what is being said and meant by various coaches and sports scientists.

Lactate threshold Lactate is a chemical compound produced in your bloodstream by exercise. The lactate level is calculated as lactate production minus any clearances. Below your lactate threshold you can clear lactate as quickly as it is produced; above it, production exceeds clearance so there are elevated levels in the blood, which you experience as fatigue. Lactate threshold is the point at which blood lactate first begins to rise above the baseline values, or in other words the intensity of exercise at which clearance no longer matches production.

Lactate is important because it determines the intensity you can sustain for prolonged

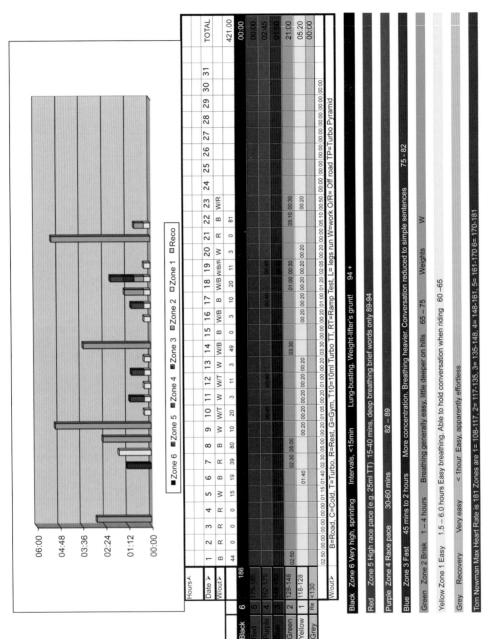

Training diary.

periods of time. Building a strong endurance base by working at this intensity helps build your ability to tolerate the training load exerted by training at higher intensities.

VO₂max This refers to the maximum amount of oxygen you can take in and use in one minute. VO_2max sets the upper limit for your aerobic performance – that is, it is the ceiling that defines your maximum aerobic ability.

You can improve your VO_2max by riding repeated three-minute intervals with three-minute recoveries. Start off with four repeats and build to eight. The key is to work at an intensity that drives your heart rate and breathing rate as high as possible.

Threshold (Functional Threshold) This is the highest average power you can maintain for one hour and signifies your highest sustainable intensity. Working beyond this level, the time you can continue riding drops off fairly rapidly. You can raise the threshold by training at this intensity but it is very demanding. Training at 90 per cent – commonly called 'sweet spot' – is intense enough to give big improvements while still allowing aerobic base development.

Max minute power In a standard fitness test known as a ramp test, the cyclist starts off at a low intensity that is then increased by a fixed amount per minute, typically 30W per minute. The highest average power that the cyclist outputs for that one minute is termed his/her max minute power. Measuring oxygen consumption during this test is the standard test for measuring VO_2max.

As a rough guide:
1.5–2W per kg of body mass = recreational rider
2–4W/kg = sportive rider
4–6 = club rider
7.5 = Alberto Contrador

You can improve your MMP by alternating riding all out for one minute with one minute of recovery.

Peak power This is the maximum instantaneous power you can produce, typically your highest five-second period. The peak value will occur at a high cadence, typically around 130rpm. It is probably best to perform a much longer sprint, maybe 12 seconds, to allow you to accelerate through a range of cadences.

Peak power is your ability to sprint, so is very important for road race riders, for example when jumping away from the bunch to attempt a break or for a final kick in a sprint. Although peak power is not too important for the time trial rider, it is worth having some sort of kick if only to outsprint your mates when racing on club runs for village signs!

As power is a product of both force and velocity – how hard you stamp on the pedals and the speed you spin them – to increase power you need to improve either or preferably both. Try standing start sprints to generate force. To improve cadence try spinning fast on low gears, ideal for turbo work. Riding fixed in the winter, especially downhill, will improve cadence as well.

Warm-Up Procedure

There have been many articles on this, with some evidence supporting the view that too hard a warm-up could be detrimental to the actual race and recommending a more gentle approach.

Going back to my friend Malcolm, he found that especially in 10-mile events, riding out for between 15 and 20 miles was an ideal warm-up and he rode his best times with this format. Failing that, I have researched and tried out many different types of warm-ups and recommend the following to all riders I coach.

Total warm-up time is 15 minutes. Firstly, gradually increase your heart rate up to 80 per cent, or a moderate effort, for 9 minutes. Then ride 5 × 30 seconds fast-paced efforts over 100rpm with 30 seconds easy spin between. Spin easy for the last minute. Then you are ready to start your training session or race.

The golden rule is the shorter the race, the longer is the warm-up. I would not advocate the above if riding a long road race or a 100-mile time trial. But certainly having a good warm-up procedure well rehearsed is beneficial for peace of mind as well as performance.

Strapped for Time

One way riders overcome minimal training time is to race a great deal. Many riders will deliberately race three times per week, which can readily be done with the number of closed road circuits available. A typical programme for a cyclist riding in this manner

Clock mounted above the turbo with second hand to gauge efforts.

would be: mid-week circuit road race and time trial typically 10 miles, one or possibly two turbo sessions slotted in somewhere and finally a weekend race. Some riders don't train during the summer; they race three times a week instead. It works for them and they've perfected this method.

There are a number of mid-week road race leagues available and the same circuits are also used for short-distance time trials. It is quite common for riders to turn up in their work attire then change into their skinsuit on site. Make it work for you if you can't find time to train. The thing to understand is there are no hard and fast rules to observe. Experiment; find out what suits you best. Are you a morning trainer or an evening one, or can you possibly fit a few sessions in at lunchtime? Analyse your week by breaking down the hours from waking to going to bed, and be realistic with the time you allocate for all the other things in your life – meals, travelling to work, work, family time and finally training time. There is always a way to slot sessions in if the motivation is sufficient, which I've found is the key.

A typical weekly training session for a time-strapped rider who wants to be competitive in 2nd/3rd category races and only has lunchtimes to train on the turbo and rides/races at weekends would be as follows. All the sessions prescribed take between 45 and 60 minutes and all riding other than the intervals and recovery within the intervals should be at an intensity that is 'uncomfortable'.

1. Fifteen 10-second max sprints with 3 minutes' recovery between each.
2. Three sets of eight 15-second max efforts, with 15 seconds recovery between efforts. Five minutes between each set of eight efforts.
3. Five 5-minute pushes at time trial effort (threshold or slightly above), with one minute recovery between each effort.

During the weekend spins, include three 5-minute time trial efforts.

Veteran Special

To stay young ride fast. It's a bit of a cliché but sometimes less is more and this is an approach that will allow you to ride hard well into your senior years. As we get older our maximum aerobic capacity (VO_2max) declines by about 5ml/kg for each year between the ages of twenty-five and sixty-five, after which the decline accelerates. However, much of the research was carried out on ordinary people: those who exercise suffer much less decline.

Your nerve fibres, which tell our muscles what to do, tend to die as we grow older.

To make matters worse, the ones connected to our bundles of fast-twitch muscle fibres tend to die out first. Once the nerve dies the muscle fibres it serves cannot be reached, so they wither away as well.

The key is to train or race in a way that fires up the fast-twitch muscle fibres, and to keep pushing at your VO_2max figure. Use it or lose it, as the saying goes. And as we advance in years we should focus more on speed and pushing hard, reducing the longer rides.

Body systems that are key are those that power a 10-second sprint, an all-out 1-minute effort, 3 minutes of hard riding plus longer efforts from 4 to 20 minutes. These efforts will preserve your fast-twitch muscle fibres and build your VO_2max. The only way you can do this is by interval training.

Key intervals are: 10-second sprints, 1

Group of riders in a winter turbo session completing 10-second sprint intervals on the turbo.

minute all-out efforts, some 3-minute intervals plus occasional longer intervals of 5 minutes or more. Ride at maximum intensity for the all-out 10-second sprints; for the 1 minute, slow down dramatically at exactly 60 seconds but not earlier; do the same for the 3 minutes. The 5-minute intervals should be ridden at a speed you can just about hold for 20 minutes.

Getting the recovery right between intervals is important and varies between each interval. For sprints the work to recovery ratio about 1:3 (so 10-second sprint is followed by 30-second recovery); for 1-minute intervals 1:2; for 3 minutes, 1:1, so for example 3 minutes on and 3 minutes off.

In one session try to ride 25 sprint efforts, ten 1-minute intervals and five 3-minute ones, but build up to this total. Getting the intensity right is the most important aspect, not the total amount of work – less is more here.

Many veteran riders don't take it too seriously. One way to remain competitive is to race against younger riders – half your age is not uncommon. Some find the only way to improve is by pushing the boundaries. Agreed, many veteran riders think they could do better, by training more smartly, eating and sleeping properly. Yet they realize they can enjoy and embrace the racing experience without going overboard. They may have a blow-out on food and drink once a week, but they have trained and raced hard and want to reward themselves. They may carry slightly too much weight and are not very competitive against much younger and considerably lighter riders but they are realistic with their expectations. For example, a road race on a pan flat course will see them hold their own, but if it is a long hilly race they may not last the distance but take pride on staying with the bunch of riders as long as possible. In training, veterans will have a friendly word with their younger, faster training friends and tell them

before they start not to wait for them if they get dropped on the hills as they will go at their own pace.

Have goals by all means but be realistic and try other aspects of the sport than road racing. It may be that a continental sportif will give you the challenge, or mountain bike racing, but keeping it fresh is a way of maintaining your enthusiasm.

Bill Butterworth – A Special Case

A West London inspiration, Bill Butterworth is, putting it kindly, over pensionable age, but competes regularly in the E/1/2/3 events at London's Hillingdon circuit. The Twickenham CC rider pushes back the boundaries with superb performances in road races against riders a third of his age.

Taking up cycling at the age of fifty-two, Bill soon blitzed through the British Cycling categories and attained his Elite category licence at the age of fifty-seven. To gain this licence, riders have to achieve 300 points in a season as 1st-category competitors.

Not content with local racing, Bill battled it out in Premier Trophy races well into his fifties. These races are currently the pinnacle of road racing in this country.

Training was a regular 12–14 hours per week with one rest day out of season, and 12 hours (including racing) with one rest day in season – all whilst working full time.

Living within striking distance of Hillingdon circuit, Bill competes regularly here. One of his biggest achievements was winning the winter league against much younger riders. Other notable achievements are: finishing UCI eight-day tour of Ireland (RAS) in 2002 aged fifty-five; numerous E/1/2 wins; silver and bronze medals in national championships; but the greatest of all was holding an Elite licence at the age of fifty-seven.

After a break of four years from serious racing he is now training hard and working his

Bill Butterworth, a supreme veteran still mixing it with the elites into his sixties.

way back to see how far up the ladder he can go at sixty-six years of age.

Thin as a pencil, Bill certainly pushes back the barriers of time and shows no signs of slowing down, an inspiration to us all.

Training for Women

There is no reason why women can't carry out the same type of training as men, and in fact many do and more successfully.

However, the menstrual cycle affects women riders by releasing variable amounts of hormones, which can affect training.

Cardiovascular, respiratory and metabolic systems are affected throughout the cycle depending on the proportion of each hormone. Some studies have shown that for performances the mid-part of the cycle was probably best, or just after menstruation, and the worst time was just before. Having said this, many records have been set by women at all stages in the menstrual cycle. Research has been conducted on individual factors, such as body temperature, glycogen utilization and strength, but at the moment there is no clear overview as to which factors seem to give an optimal time for performance.

Women's circuit race.

Women mixing it with men at the finish – sixth over the line.

Poles Hill in the Chilterns, a Strava hill (see Chapter 7).

Ideally the training programme would be arranged so that menstruation coincides with the easy training week. Of course women can't control when their menstrual cycle occurs but the use of contraceptive pills may be an option to control oestrogen levels. Consult your doctor first before taking any course of action.

Special Disciplines

Hill Climbing

We all want to be better climbers and there are countless sessions that you can practise to maximize your performance. Whatever you do, it will be painful – hills certainly hurt. Many events we ride include hills and being able to stay with attacks or indeed initiate them requires you to climb well and incur pain, so you may as well get used to it.

An interval session that follows a format of easy/medium/hard is going to get very painful as the session gets progressively more nasty.

A good hill climb session would be to select a hill of medium grade (about 6–8 per cent), which takes anywhere between 3 and 10 minutes to ride up. Split the hill into three zones.

1: Ride the first 50 per cent of the hill at a rate of perceived exertion (RPE) of 7 out of 10.

2: Ride the next 30 per cent of the hill at an RPE of 8.

Honking up a hill: riders showing good style and maintaining an intense effort with bikes well under control.

Riders climbing a hill in an early season sportif.

3: Ride the final 20 per cent of the hill at an RPE of 9.

When riding the hill focus on perceptible step-ups in intensity between the three stages and, if feeling good, add in a fourth, which is a full-on RPE 10 sprint over the top of the hill for the final 20m when you are completing the first set in a fresh condition.

Recover by spinning back easily to the bottom of the hill and repeating it all over again two or three times. You can make it more interesting by varying the gradient and length. You may want to practise riding the first set in the saddle, second set out of the saddle and the third set a combination of both.

Remember RPE is subjective – a measure of how hard you think the effort is: 7 is tough, 8 is uncomfortably hard and 9 is when you think it can't possibly be any harder. Of course 10 is a maximum, full-on sprint effort.

Sprinting

Most road races, though not all, are won with a sprint, especially the circuit events run on closed circuits. So being good at sprinting, compared to your competitors, gives you a big advantage in the closing stages of a race and is also very useful if you have to bridge gaps, or indeed break away without towing the entire field with you.

Like climbers, sprinters are born, not made, and a product of their genes. Normally sprinters will be more heavily muscled and equipped with a high proportion of muscle fibres (maybe 75 per cent) of type II white, fast-twitch muscle fibres. These fibres have a high anaerobic capacity but low aerobic capacity. Put simply, they provide explosive power and high top-end speed but fatigue quickly.

As a road rider aiming to improve your anaerobic capacity, you train for sprinting by sprinting. Practise by sprinting from a fast rolling start by riding in a high gear for 10–15 seconds flat out. Recover by riding gently for three minutes and repeating again six to ten times. Although not terribly fatiguing, this training drill is surprisingly effective.

Another good session is to find a road with a dip either side. Hurtle down one side and go flat out on a high gear up the other side. Rest for a minute or two and repeat in the other direction, and again repeat the exercise for a total six to ten times.

It is important to avoid wasting energy by not throwing your bike all over the road, keeping elbows tucked in and arms pulling up, not outwards. Practise sprinting as often as possible, both in and out of the saddle. Work on explosive power as well by jumping as hard as you can in a high gear.

In a race the way to sprint will vary considerably according to the circumstances and the strengths of the riders around you. If you can get a lead out then all well and good, but don't be afraid to go from the front. With indexed geared systems it's much easier to change up whilst hurtling towards the line.

Bunch sprint for the line at the end of an early season circuit race.

Tapering

Before a big targeted event is essential that you avoid tiredness and arrive fresh. An ideal taper is one that produces lots of rest but very little detraining. Five rules to follow to achieve a good taper are as follows:

- The taper period should last a week.
- Reduce the total amount of training by about 50 per cent, so if you normally spend 8 hours per week training then reduce to 4 hours.
- Frequency of training should remain unchanged.
- The intensity should remain high as before.
- All activities should be specific to the discipline – in other words, no running, long walks, swimming or playing other sports to avoid muscle injuries.

Getting the taper right is difficult, as can be seen with our Olympic athletes. You want to arrive at the start line raring to go but not tired from your previous schedule.

Psychology

Tensions can arise when competing. You can make a choice to act positively or negatively.

By acting positively you fight the reaction and embrace the challenge.

By choosing this reaction, you don't have to get aggressive but direct your energies towards the task in hand. For example, determine to do a good ride and give the race your utmost. You will be unconcerned about the weather and take what comes.

By acting negatively, you may be overpowered by the situation you've found yourself in. Some riders will withdraw, think about possible troubles, like crashing or bike problems, weather conditions and their rivals' strength. Thinking like this is the start of a downward spiral and the result will be poor.

Some riders will aspire to tackle new hurdles, determined to overcome them. From a coaching point of view it is difficult to predict riders' attitudes. Some riders are simply good trainers but poor racers. Other riders simply hate training and have to be forced out, but put them on a start line and they are fierce competitors. This type of rider is motivated by the challenge and gets strength from this, with the thought of medals and perhaps wealth being the ultimate goal.

Wrong Word at the Wrong Time

At time trials most top riders avoid people before the start. They are psyching themselves up for the race, concentrating their thoughts on the imminent ride. They don't want to make small talk and potentially be irritated by some thoughtless comment. As an example, if it is raining the last thing you want to hear is some remark pointing out the conditions and the increased chance of crashing. Avoid this tension and simply focus on the race and what you are going to do.

Who Are You?

Sports psychology is a big subject and an entire book could be devoted to it. For the amateur racing cyclist it is simply a matter of trying to get the best out of yourself with the time and resources you have available.

So what sort of rider are you? It is worth spending a bit of time analysing this. For example, are you motivated by the situation that confronts you or would you rather be somewhere else?

Avoid negative thoughts and focus on success. Assuming your training and diet are correct, that you are sleeping well and your bike is in tip-top shape, there is every reason to expect that you can succeed.

Performance Analysis

If, despite your best efforts, you don't reach the level you want to reach, then try self-analysis. After each race have a good, long look at what happened and study your performance realistically to see where it went wrong. Look at this objectively. It may have been your warm-up, not concentrating, the break may have gone while you were looking at your computer, or you went too fast initially in a time trial.

Your strengths still develop, but work on your weaknesses. It may be hill climbing, for example; you may not be the lightest rider in the world, but many riders who win hilly races are not either, so don't let this be a detriment to your performance. Another perceived weak-

ness may be that you are nervous in bunches, so rubbing shoulders with team mates in training (safely, preferably, on a closed circuit) will get you used to this situation.

Develop this area of your training, working on your weaknesses, so that you become more confident. The knowledge that you are physically well prepared and equipped with a positive mental attitude will give you the self-confidence to turn out good performances.

Bombard Your Fitness

Perhaps winter training hasn't gone too well and the best-laid plans of mice and men have gone awry. A mild panic is rising inescapably as your programme of events is looming up on the horizon. So what to do?

Bombard your fitness by tackling a short, intense three- to four-week fitness programme to perk up your systems and bring them up to speed. The schedule consists of three weeks of intense work followed by an easy week. It is tough, though, so don't use it too much because you can overtrain on less than 6 hours of training per week.

Warm-up Every workout should be proceeded with a 10- to 15-minute warm-up and followed by a cool down for a similar period.

Stretching/core workout See Chapter 5.

Hill intervals These are ridden on a steep hill that takes about 2 minutes to climb. Ride the hill as hard as you can and note the time. Turn around at the top, recover on the descent. Repeat five to ten times.

VO_2max intervals These last 3 minutes, at the greatest intensity you can maintain at a constant effort for the entire 3 minutes. Try to ride three VO_2max intervals but no more than five. Take 3 minutes' recovery with easy pedalling between efforts.

Three-week boost for fitness

	Monday	Tuesday	Wednesday	Thursday	Friday	Saturday	Sunday
Week I Training workouts	Stretching/ core work	Ride at AT (anaerobic threshold) for 20min	Hill intervals	Endurance ride 1–1.5hr	Stretching/ core work	5 x 5min at AT with 4min recovery between, easy spinning	Endurance ride, minimum 2hr at higher level Z2/lower-level Z3
Week 2 Training workouts	Stretching/ core work	4 x 2.5 miles at AT, 4min recovery between each block	Long intervals: 15min at 20 per cent below AT, 15min at 10 per cent below AT and 15min at AT	VO$_2$max intervals	Stretching/ core work	Hill intervals	Endurance ride
Week 3 Training workouts	Stretching/ core work	1min intervals	Endurance ride	20/40s	Stretching/ core work	Sprint session	Endurance ride

One-minute max intervals These are similar to VO$_2$ intervals except you are riding as hard as you can for 1 minute. Initially aim for five, with ten the limit. It is important that you spread your effort evenly over the entire duration. Starting off too fast and fading is not the way to tackle this workout. You should run out of breath about 5 seconds from the end and hang on for these final few seconds.

Anaerobic threshold (AT) These workouts are ridden at a pace you could keep up for 1 hour, typically a 25-mile time trial pace.

20/40s These are best ridden on a turbo trainer. Ride as hard as you can for 20 seconds, recover by pedalling easy for 40 seconds and repeat a total of five times. Recover for 4 minutes then ride two more sets with the same recovery period between.

Sprint workouts These are unadulterated sprinting and can be incorporated into a longer ride if required. Ride on a flat, safe stretch of road in as big a gear as you can handle, and take 5 minutes recovery between each sprint. Visualize yourself in front of a baying pack of riders lunging for the line.

Endurance ride Ride for a minimum of 2 hours at upper-level Z2/lower-level Z3 pace.

Set aside quality rest time, as the specified training period needs you to push hard for one three-day and one two-day chunk of training. Concentrate fully on each session and on the entire three-week programme. If you have a busy time at work coming up or a full calendar of family engagements then don't attempt this, as it will be too difficult and you won't get the intended benefits.

Stamina, power and speed are functions of cycling fitness. This fitness bombardment tackles all three of these. Speed and power are built with short efforts whilst power and stamina are constructed with longer efforts. In the three-week programme the sessions are set out so that they complement each other and generally move from longer to shorter efforts.

Key systems that power cycling include full-on sprint sessions to strike fast-twitch muscle and build raw speed. Short intervals are used to build power and longer intervals to increase your cruising speed. Stamina is built with endurance rides. All of your aptitudes are built up in a short space of time with this training programme.

Many professional racers train this way so this schedule is quite similar to theirs. Training in this manner allows them to focus on each fundamental aspect – speed, power and stamina – that they will need for their racing. In road racing, for example, two essential characteristics are the ability to initiate and maintain attacks. So to improve your speed and anaerobic threshold (maximum level of effort for one hour) several sessions are included that focus specifically on this.

In your riding there may be some areas you are less proficient in – say hill climbing or pace judging – and this programme addresses these issues too.

Many racing cyclists who are habitually strapped for time train like this throughout the year. They don't necessarily hit an achievement high but then conversely they don't suffer from lows either. However, the tried and tested method of periodization – selecting objectives and then training accordingly – is generally regarded as a superior approach to training. Rack up a good endurance base and then use interval training to hone your ability to ride hard for shorter periods.

For those riders who select a few events throughout the year, such as a 12-hour event when they want to ride in a team with other team mates, the periodization method will be more effective.

This doesn't mean you shouldn't still identify weaknesses in your riding. Say, for example, that on club rides with your friends you find yourself clicking through the gears on hills desperately seeking a suitable combination of ratios whilst they disappear up the road. To improve this aspect of your riding, you would pick out from this schedule the hill climbing aspect and specifically practise this skill. After a few weeks noting your times on your test hill coming down, your confidence will have improved and you should be able to stay amongst the cluster of your club mates' wheels when tackling the hills on your rides.

Whilst trying to ride the entire three-week programme, you can use the various sessions as you see fit. You can even use some of the various sessions within your periodization programme to perk up your training as you see

A winter-cross rider tackling the course.

Start of the National Cyclo Cross championships for veteran men in Birmingham.

fit. Of course, whatever you decide to cherry pick from this schedule has to be appropriate for the type of event you are riding. If most of your events require you to be riding for over 4 hours at a steady speed like a sportif, there is no point in selecting sprint work.

Every characteristic aspect of your riding can be incorporated into this programme to give your cycling a shot in the arm. But don't be anything less than committed and give your riding precedence to make the most of the benefits. Take care of obvious nutritional needs and ensure you get quality rest so that you recover from the sessions well and are fresh and raring to go to tackle the next session.

Training in the Off Season: Running

In the gloomy days and nights of winter, riding your bike is often challenging and you may tire from endless turbo sessions. Getting out in the fresh air is a tonic in itself and that is where running comes in: it is hard to beat for cheapness, ease and time-efficiency.

Furthermore, unlike other activities or sports, such as swimming, Pilates, yoga, indoor tennis or badminton, it is something we all can do. Even so, it is possible to injure yourself, so before strapping the trainers on and heading out of the front door, you need to observe a few simple rules.

Cycling and running are different. Although you use the same muscles and both are aerobic activities, the way you are propelled is different. Muscular forces in cycling drive the pedals around. With running you land on the ground and the energy of impact is absorbed into the tendons and muscles. This energy is then released so you thrust forward. The impact is the crucial difference and determines the way you train.

With cycling, you can ride for long periods and push on the pedals quite hard without any undue consequences. Rides of less than one hour don't seem worth the effort of donning the lycra. Running, on the other hand, unless you are very experienced, will not allow that, with the impact involved. But don't let this put you off; you simply have to observe a few golden rules.

Start off with short runs If, on your first foray, you attempt an hour's run, or even half an hour, you run a ludicrous risk of injury. On your first run aim for 10–15 minutes and preferably on grass to lessen the impact even further. To make matters even easier insert walk breaks randomly into the workout.

Little and often Four 20- to 30-minute runs per week are much better and more prudent than two longer runs of over 60 minutes. In longer runs, impact damage plus weariness cumulate, increasing the possibility of injuring yourself, and your muscles will be sore. You often hear of new runners complaining of hamstrings like concrete when they overdo it.

In any case your running fitness will certainly improve more efficiently if you exercise in frequent sessions.

Take it easy Many sports scientists advocate increasing your running by only 10 per cent per week maximum. Any more will dramatically increase your chances of being injured. Keep your effort easy and relaxed rather than running really hard. You should be able to speak in short sentences.

Select a good route It should ideally be flat. Running on steep downhill sections is likely to double the risk of injury compared to the flat, though running uphill is fine. The terrain needs to be smooth, so avoid rough surfaces. Lastly, as mentioned above, the ground should be soft, such as short grass; football pitches are ideal, or failing that smooth tarmac or trails.

Running carries a higher risk of muscle damage than cycling, and it needs to be done frequently. By running two to three times per week regularly you will receive the full bene-fits. Take one or two days off between days of running – you can still cycle on those days. If you intend to run and cycle on the same day, then run first.

Regarding equipment, seek out a good running shop. Many have a running machine installed so that they can track your footfall and recommend the best type of running shoe. A good shoe is likely to cost anything from £60 to £100 but it is worth it. If you are only running on grass it may be best to select a cross-training shoe, which has sole grips to hold the terrain more firmly and avoid slipping.

To sum up, running will make you a fitter, better-conditioned, improved athlete overall. Many riders feel the benefit of regular running even when on the bike and as a high-quality session it cannot be faulted. A rider from my club, even in the height of time trial season, has a couple of lunchtime runs of about 3 miles and still manages to trot out 21-minute 10-mile and 54-minute 25-mile cycle races.

Running workout plan for 10 weeks

Week	Number 1 run	Number 2 run	Number 3 run
1	10 x 2min run with 1min walk between each effort	6 x 3min run with 1min walk between each effort	5 x 4min run with 1min walk between each effort
2	5 x 5min run with 1min walk between each effort	3 x 6min run with 1min walk between each effort	3 x 7min run with 1min walk between each effort
3	2 x 9min run with 2min walk in between	2 x 10min run with 2min walk in between	2 x 10min run with 1min walk in between
4	12min run, then 1min walk, then 8min run	15min run, then 1min walk, then 5min run	20min run
5	20min run	20min run	20min run
6	22min run	22min run	22min run
7	24min run	24min run	24min run
8	26min run	26min run	26min run
9	28min run	28min run	28min run
10	30min run	30min run	30min run

Road Racing Licence Categories

All junior and senior licence holders, male or female are categorized by their ability. Riders of the same ability category compete together in races, irrespective of their age category, except in the case of age-related events.

Senior Riders

4th Category A new junior or senior licence holder.

3rd Category Any junior or senior licence holder who has gained 10 points during any one season whilst holding a 4th category licence. Note: Riders are never downgraded to 4th category once a 3rd category licence has been achieved.

2nd Category Any junior or senior licence holder who has gained 40 points during any one season whilst holding a 3rd category licence. To retain a 2nd category licence for the following season, a rider must obtain at least 25 points in events open to that category of rider.

1st Category Any junior or senior licence holder who has gained 200 points during any one season whilst holding a 2nd category licence. To retain a 1st category licence for the following season, a rider must obtain at least 100 points in events open to that category of rider.

Elite Category Any rider who: has gained 300 points during the previous season whilst holding an elite or 1st category licence; or, at 31 December of the previous year was listed in the top 10 in the Senior Men's National Cross Country MTB Rankings.

Junior Riders

On reaching the Junior age category, existing licence holders will be awarded initial ability categories as follows:

4th Category Any rider who has gained no Youth licence points in the previous year.

3rd Category Any rider who has gained Youth licence points in the previous year.

2nd Category male Any rider who has achieved: Top 15 in the Youth A Boys in the previous year's National Circuit Race Series; or Top 10 in the Youth A Boys in the previous year's Track Omnium Series; or Top 3 in any in the previous year's Road/Track Youth A Boys National Championship; or Top 10 in Youth A Boys National Rankings in the previous season.

2nd Category female Any rider who has achieved: Top 5 in the Youth A Girls in the previous year's National Circuit Race Series; or Top 10 in the Youth A Girls in the previous year's Track Omnium Series; or Top 3 in any in the previous year's Road/Track Youth A Girls National Championship; or Top 5 in Youth A Girls National Rankings in the previous season.

Note: Junior riders are not be eligible for elite licences

Event Classification System

The event classification system for road and circuit racing was introduced in 2006. Aimed at increasing the opportunities to race and the relevance of the racing, the system breaks events down into two main categories – national and regional – and is linked to national, regional, club and team rankings. Road and circuit events, other than those exclusively for youth, juniors, women and masters, are classified as follows.

National A

Eligibility Open to Senior male elite, 1st and 2nd category riders with a Full Racing Licence.

National A closed road circuit events shall also be open to 1st and 2nd category junior riders.

Distance/time
- Single day event: minimum 130km if terrain is demanding; maximum of 180km on flatter terrain.
- Road stage of stage race: minimum 80km.
- Circuit race: minimum time 60 minutes, and maximum 90 minutes.

Prize list The main prize list shall be a minimum of £2,000. Prize money shall be paid to riders placed at least 1st to 20th.

Note: Only one National A event shall be held on the same day in the UK.

National B

Eligibility Open to Senior male elite, 1st, 2nd and 3rd category riders, final year Junior male 1st, 2nd and 3rd category and Senior female elite 1st and 2nd category riders with a Full Racing Licence. Where the minimum distance for a road race is not achieved, the race shall be open to all Junior male 1st, 2nd and 3rd category riders and all Junior female 1st and 2nd category riders. For National B closed circuit events, all 1st, 2nd and 3rd category Juniors are eligible to ride.

Distance/time
- Single day event: minimum 120km (where the race is less than 120km, it will be dropped by 1 points band).
- Circuit race: minimum time 60 minutes.

Regional A

Eligibility Open to Senior and Junior male 2nd, 3rd and 4th category and Senior and Junior female riders of all categories with a Full Racing Licence or holders of a Day Licence.

Distance/time
- Single day event: minimum 80km.
- Circuit race: minimum time 50 minutes.

Regional B

Eligibility Open to Senior and Junior male 3rd and 4th category riders and Senior and Junior female riders of all categories with a Full Racing Licence or holders of a Day Licence.

Distance/time
- Single day event: maximum 90km.
- Circuit race: minimum time 40 minutes.

Regional C and Regional C+

Eligibility Open to Senior and Junior riders of all categories with a Full Racing Licence or holders of a Day Licence. Race to be run as a handicap or other appropriate format. Race may also be restricted to 4th category riders only, or holders of a Day Licence.

Distance/time The minimum time shall be 30 minutes, and the maximum 90 minutes

Notes: Where the circuit is too small to allow for a handicap event that meets the minimum time requirement, the organizer may choose to use an alternative format, provided that the chosen format reasonably caters for the widest possible range of ability. Time Trials shall be run as Regional C+ or Regional C events.

Go Race
An introductory level of racing open to 4th category riders with a Full Racing Licence, British Cycling Provisional Licence holders and non-members.

Distance/time The maximum time for a Go-Race event shall be 30 minutes.

CHAPTER 3

Techniques and Tactics

Road Racing

Riding in a Group

One of the biggest problems new riders face when starting road racing is riding closely to the other riders at high speeds. Many newcomers to the sport don't necessarily belong to clubs that on their club runs instil a discipline into their riding – for example, riding at the correct distance to the back wheel of the rider in front and to the rider next to them. So skills are picked up whilst on the open road and mistakes are most of the time pointed out to them in a friendly manner. It is much better to pick up these skills amongst friends than in an actual race, where you may accidentally carve up your fellow competitors and suffer a tongue-lashing for your efforts.

These basic skills have to be learned first. If you don't belong to a good club – and I advocate this – then try to either seek out coach-led training sessions or rustle up a group of riders. Aim for a similar level to yourself and organize a training session. A closed circuit is best but, failing that, maybe a quite factory estate or quiet roads with all left-hand turns. An ideal distance would be about 1–2 miles so you are lapping regularly and taking lots of corners.

Practise rubbing shoulders but not too hard to start off with. Get used to the feel of a large, fast-moving group, as shown in the picture.

Start of a circuit road race.

Bunch approaching a corner, taking good racing lines.

This is part and parcel of road racing and also learning the art of 'holding a wheel'. By being able to hold a wheel in two-up formation travelling at 25mph you may save up to 30 per cent energy. In the middle of a bunch the savings could be as great as 40 per cent.

There are some golden rules to observe. First, never overlap the rear wheel of the rider in front of you, unless you are riding in a close staggered formation because of a crosswind. Try instead to keep a minimum of about 15cm (6in) behind the wheel and similar distance to one side, so you have space to ride up the side of their wheel should they slow down. Your front wheel is the one to worry about. If someone touches your back wheel (even at speed) it will rarely result in a crash for you, but your front wheel affects the bike's steering so that is the one to keep out of trouble.

In your training sessions, practise riding in team time trial formation one behind the other, where all of you are concentrating on the wheel in front. After riding this drill a few times you will be much more accomplished at holding a wheel in front and concentrating

hard. After a few more sessions, learn to look further ahead than the wheel you are following. Look ahead for obstacles in the road, and changes in race direction. Your peripheral vision will allow you to be aware of the position of your front wheel in relation to the other riders.

It helps if you can watch a high-level town centre race near you and see the riders demonstrating cycling skills at the top level. See how close they ride to each other at high speed while maintaining the correct distance between bikes, and the level of confidence with which they handle their bikes.

Many crashes occur in road racing when riders get out of the saddle wrongly. This can easily be avoided if you learn to get out of the saddle smoothly, pressing a bit harder on the pedals as you do so. It is a common mistake riders make when they get out of the saddle to ease off the pedals, resulting in the bike slowing momentarily. If you do this and the rider behind you is not switched on to what's happening and touches your rear wheel with his front wheel, he may lose balance and crash, possibly bringing some more riders down with him. Alternatively, you could be

*Good style out
of the saddle,
focused on the
road ahead.*

the rider whose front wheel touches the rear wheel in front with the resultant carnage. In a line of riders, try to get out of the saddle when at the end of the string, rather than in the middle.

Learn to keep a good, straight line, avoiding unnecessary sudden changes of direction. Practise this in your training and also try to relax while doing so, while still maintaining your concentration. It's not uncommon in races to be complimented on your riding skills by your competitors, who may comment on how rock steady you are and what a safe wheel to follow. Some riders do notice.

Position in the bunch is important if you are to ride at your best and avoid the many problems that may arise. Some riders think that by

riding at the rear of the group they will avoid working hard, by getting more 'drag' and as a result having an easier race. This is not actually the case in practice.

The accepted best spot is in the first fifteen to twenty riders in a field of sixty or more. In this position you will always be well placed to answer and create attacks where the action is.

A higher percentage of crashes occurs in the rear part of the field. Leading riders tend to be more focused, want to race and are automatically aware of what is going on around them. Riders at the tail of the bunch tend to be those who are looking for an easier ride, or ones who are more tired and so lack concentration – an ideal recipe for crash victims.

There is one exception. In some circuit races, some riders, unable to break away and sprint for the line from a small group, give up on a placing, deeming it too risky getting involved in a mass swirling bunch sprint with a greater chance of a crash. So with a lap or two to go, they slowly drift back through the bunch and watch the action from a safe distance just off the back.

Climbing

Climbing is an important technique in road racing. Many breaks are formed either on the actual climb or just over the summit, where there is a slack in the pace with riders taking a breather.

Though innate climbing ability is often down to hereditary factors, you will generally find that a rider with a good power to weight ratio can manage to get over the climbs well. If you are not blessed with superior climbing skills fear not, they can be improved. Two main factors come into play: rider weight and their power to weight ratio.

One of the most efficient ways to climb is with your hands on the 'tops'. Climb with a wide grip, pulling on the bars to give your legs a resistance to oppose. Aim to climb rhythmically, and when out of the saddle, honking. Hold the brake lever hoods (the photo on page 47 shows two riders in the front honking, one on top of the levers one on the drops), moving the saddle from side to side but keeping your body in a straight line. When honking in this fashion, you are in effect pulling up on the handlebars on the same side as the descending pedal, using the power of your shoulders to augment the strength of your thighs in pushing the pedal down. It's the same principle you use when pulling on your wellingtons.

Train yourself to breathe slowly and deeply when climbing, avoiding quick shallow breathing.

Start the hill at the front of the group, and then if the pace is too quick for you, you'll slip back through the riders and be on the tail by the time the group reaches the top.

Don't change chainrings on the climb. Changing up from the small ring to the large ring can be tricky under pressure, and changing down can be disastrous. If you elect to stay on the big ring, and change down through the sprockets until you're on the largest 21 and then find you need a lower gear, you're at the point where the chain is running across from the biggest sprocket to the bigger ring at an acute angle. At the same time you are pushing hard on the pedals, so when you change down the chain could easily miss the smaller ring and drop off. This is no fun when you're going uphill.

In training, practise hill techniques. Try to do a certain amount of training with other riders, especially ones who are better climbers than you. Keep changes in your pace to a minimum to avoid 'dead legs'.

Hills are a natural place to attack. The speed is slower than on the flat, therefore minimizing slipstreaming, so you can even attack from a leading position (a mistake in other circumstances) and open a gap if you are strong enough. As mentioned above, one of the best moments to attack is across the top of a climb. Riders who have reacted to attacks on a climb are at their limit, or simply struggling with the gradient, tend to measure their effort to the top, knowing life will get easier on the descent. Therefore launching an attacking move when a climb is all but over is very effective. A steep climb, easing just before the top, and a good section of flat before the ensuing descent are an ideal combination to make your move if you can.

Attacking this way is no great surprise move as every rider expects it. None the less they still don't want to react and would prefer if someone else did the chasing. If everyone leaves the chase to someone else, nobody chases, and you open a gap in no time.

Try not to:

- Approach the climb in too high a gear
- Be too far back in the bunch
- Wrongly anticipate the length or gradient of the climb and ride too hard on the early part of the climb
- Miss opportunities to close gaps and move back through the bunch when approaching the top of the climb
- Get too close to the rider in front and have to slow down if riding on a weaker rider's wheel
- Grip the bars too tightly and rock back and forth in the saddle.

Descending

Some of the world's best climbers are poor descenders, so take some encouragement from that.

One professional rider a few years ago took to listening to classical music to sooth his nerves and apparently it worked, but I don't advocate the use of this method as it is vital to keep all your senses alert.

When descending, whether in a group or racing bunch, it is important to be relaxed and alert.

Try to:

- Hold your handlebars by the drops, covering the brakes
- Leave a small gap between yourself and other riders to give you a clear sight of any obstructions in front, and keep your head up
- Ride smoothly in and out of corners; try to identify the best line to take that will give you an opportunity to overtake in one go before any tight bends
- Maybe identify a 'safe rider' – note their number and follow them down the climb
- Conversely, avoid dodgy riders whose bike skills are suspect.

Taking a sharp corner before a climb.

Descending fast, two riders making an escape from the bunch.

Try not to:

- Adopt an extreme aerodynamic position
- Descend beyond your limitations, thus compromising your own and other riders' safety
- Fail to notice the rider in front's racing line and as a result having to brake excessively
- Follow a slower descender than you or a rider whose technique is inferior to yours.

Braking

Know your brakes well and ensure they are adjusted the same across all your bikes, both training and racing. As braking is instinctive, you can expect the same result when you use them.

It takes great energy to get up to speed, so don't waste this by braking unnecessarily. During a race try to brake conservatively,

instead easing up pedalling. If a hazard looms up start to brake gently by squeezing the levers, and only put on the anchors really hard if you have to. Modern dual-calliper brakes are very powerful and it's very easy to lock the wheels, especially the rear.

Spread the braking over both front and rear. Ensure you can easily reach the brake levers by positioning them correctly. A front brake judder suggests a loose headset. If this is not the problem, check the rim for a buckle or dents. Likewise, a front wheel judder suggests a buckle or damaged rim.

Do not:

- Apply brakes excessively and too hard
- Use only one brake instead of both.

Cornering

Cornering at speed normally causes heartache for beginners. With only a few square

Bunch showing good cornering technique.

centimetres of rubber in contact with the road, a bicycle is actually remarkably stable, assuming you don't try to dissuade it too much from a straight line.

The picture shows a good example of riders entering and exiting the bend in a circuit race. The key to fast and safe cornering is to eliminate the corner of the bend as much as you can and ride in as straight a line as possible.

The more you turn the handlebars the more your front wheel, under gyroscopic force, will try to turn them back. The bike likes to be ridden in a straight line. So the worst way to enter a corner is to ride straight up to the bend, brake hard at the last moment, pull the bars round and hug the inside of the bend. With this method you will lose lengths on

every corner and have to put in a large effort to regain the wheels in front. On a fifty-lap circuit race with four corners each lap – 200 corners – you won't have much left if indeed you reach the finish.

Cornering is something you can practise in training. Try following a more experienced rider and watch closely the line they take.

The fastest way through a corner is not necessarily the shortest. Take a 90-degree left-hand bend as an example.

The correct technique is to move out to the right as you approach the bend: either to the crown of the road, racing under normal conditions, or even further if it's a closed circuit. Fix your line, go into the corner at the correct speed, and accelerate out of the corner. Brake before the corner – not on it. Once you've

Fast corner technique going up a hill.

got your line, try to look at where you want to go rather than at the nearside kerb. If you concentrate on looking at the kerb you'll find your bike won't be going where you intended, you'll attempt a sudden change of direction and could well land up in a heap. Lean your bike into the corner, keeping your inside foot up and the outside one down. Move your weight over your inside knee into the corner. This slight shift helps your bike turn. Aim your bike (competitors willing) to cut across the apex of the bend, as this is the shortest route through it. Once out of the corner and going straight, get out of the saddle to ensure you accelerate quickly.

If you encounter a sharp corner, so you are unable to pedal through it and need to freewheel, transfer your weight to the outside pedal; this lowers your centre of gravity, thus giving maximum tyre adhesion. Watch the riders in front carefully to see what technique they adopt going through the bend. Are they braking, are they pedalling? This will prepare you for deciding on your actions.

Gear Changing

Using gears correctly is based on much the same principle as in cars. An engine performs best at certain revs, just like cadence. You are at your most efficient at optimum rpm. If you start to labour, then it's time to change, but as a general rule it's better to change gear too early than too late. Change gears quickly and efficiently.

Try to:

- Increase cadence before changing to a higher gear
- Know the course so you have an idea of when to change gears
- Use gears to maintain a constant cadence, especially over hills normally above 80rpm.

In circuit races especially change to an easier gear to allow rapid acceleration out of a corner.

Try not to:

- Select an inappropriate range of gears for the event

- Use too high a gear when climbing, which will force you to ride at greater intensity than is desirable
- Wrongly anticipate the need to change gear, so you leave it too late and lose time, momentum and position in the bunch
- Let cadence drop before changing to a lower gear
- Flag your attacking intentions by changing gear and then attacking; it's better to attack first then change gear.

Sprinting

Many races are decided in a sprint finish. They can be long or short sprints, from a small group who have broken away or in a large bunch. Whilst every rider can't pretend to be Mark Cavendish, you should seek to improve your sprint in training.

In most road or circuit races in the UK lead-out tactics as seen in the Tour de France won't be used. Normally there is little or no supporting team involvement, so the actual sprint can be very short indeed: no single rider wants to act as lead-out man for the rest and consequently ruin their chances. What happens instead is that the break goes slower and slower until someone's nerve cracks.

Whether sprinting from a big bunch or from a small group, certain principles apply. First, stay in the most sheltered position for as long as possible, which means finding a good wheel to follow (preferably your targeted opponents). Move out into the wind only to make your effort. It's a good idea to practise this in training with mates and see what a difference it makes.

The finishing sprint is often but not always the highest speed during a race, so wind resistance is a big factor. Be aware not only which is the best wheel to come off but from which side the wind is blowing, so you can try to come off the sheltered side.

The second principle is correct gear selection before starting your sprint. Consider the variables, such as whether the wind is against you, if it is a uphill finish and the distance from the last corner; you may want to gear down. On the other hand, if there is a bunch sprint at the end of a long straight on flat or descending roads, then you should gear up. Trying to change gear once you've launched your effort is fatal, as a missed gear change at high speed can have unattractive consequences.

Third, make sure you have somewhere to go. Don't allow too many riders in front of

Fast sprint for the line.

Two riders making a positive attempt at breaking away.

you for the wind-up to the finish. The riders in front will not graciously move out of the way to allow you to go past them! Be aware of the opposition and work out where in the bunch the good sprinters are. If one should make an early move, too early in your opinion, try to get over onto their wheel.

If you can, place yourself where you won't be forced into the wind. Good bunch positioning skills come into play at this point. Assess your ability compared to your rivals. If you think you are the strongest and the finish is either up a hill or into the wind, then launch a long sprint. This should hopefully tire out the specialists who would normally win in a shorter contest.

Conversely, if you are tired but a talented sprinter then do your utmost to engineer a short sprint. Many sprinters can be seen yo-yoing at the back of the group only to come alive at the finish and win with a short devastating sprint. This is why the strongest rider does not always necessarily win.

If you've decided you haven't a hope, then go for a long one before anyone expects it, certainly before the 200m to go sign. Maybe the sprinters figure you will fade and concentrate too hard on watching each other, thus enabling you to win; it has happened.

Making a Break

A road race can be separated into various bouts of activity. Early on it's frisky but not serious; after this period the race is really on and attacks have an intensity and eagerness about them. The seriousness of the pursuit matches the seriousness of the attack, as a result of bigger players judging it is now time to attack, join or counter the efforts of other attackers.

Crits-bunch.

Attacks are often initiated by hills, stretches of rough roads, crashes or weather conditions, such as the wind. Once an attack has succeeded in opening a serious margin – over a minute – activity in the bunch often settles down into a strong chasing effort or resignation, acknowledging the break will stay away. Towards the finish there is an increase in activity, with those riders who do not relish sprinting against their perceived better sprinting rivals trying to steal away. Sometimes there is a lull before the break gets ready to wind up for the final sprint.

This is all predictable, but the good tactician and alert rider will pick the correct moment to attack and not bring with them a big chasing effort. Undoubtedly the best time to attack is when the majority of riders are less inclined to chase, for example:

- When a dangerous breakaway is about to be caught after a hard chase. With the gap reduced to a few metres, sprint across and keep your effort going. You might be fortunate and pick up some of the stronger break's riders while the slowing riders may hinder the bunch, stopping reactions.
- Just before, or just over the top of a climb, when the bunch slows after making a big effort on the climb; if a long descent follows, however, any advantage gained may be negated.
- When there is a crash. On the face of it this seems unsporting, but looked at another way, your superior bunch positioning skills presented you with this opportunity, so give it everything.
- When the roads are narrow and twisting and the bunch is strung out. Many riders, especially at the back, won't see you escape.
- On a bend, either just before or just after – once again only the front riders will see this move.

Race Craft

Older and more experienced roadmen who are past their best can often survive with younger rivals by riding more cleverly – for example, taking shelter from the wind, relaxing whenever possible and only making an effort when they have to.

Riding on a wheel, taking shelter in this manner, saves a lot of energy – as much as 30 per cent in some cases. Be careful of overlapping wheels. If your front wheel is overlapping the rider in front's rear wheel and he should move sideways, he will swipe your front wheel; he won't feel a thing but you most likely will

Good example of a time trial position.

crash as both your balance and steering will be badly affected. So always keep a close eye on wheels and give yourself a margin of safety.

Time Trialling

This is the 'race of truth' as the French call it. There's no hiding in time trials: just you, machine and the course, no excuses. The winner is the person who can go fastest or furthest over the designated course. Great Britain has a long history in this discipline of the sport, harking back to an age when racing, especially massed start, on the open road was frowned on. Time trialling was run on courses given code numbers (no road numbers were mentioned) to confuse the local police and events were held very early in the morning, normally Sundays.

The set distances in Britain have a big fan base and the popularity of these events outstrips road racing. Set distances are 10, 25, 30 (not so popular now), 50 and 100 miles. Time trials are also run over 12 or 24 hours, where it is the distance covered that counts.

Now all major road championships have a separate time trial championship and of course the major tours have time trial stages, from prologues, which are very short distances, to longer distances such as 40km. A rider who does well in time trials as well as being competitive in most of the other road race aspects has a distinct advantage; for example,

NO	NAME	START TIME H/CAP	SCRATCH TIME	H/CAP TIME	POSN P.T.P.
1.	ANNIE BIRCH				
2.	IAN BIRCH WILLESDEN CC	9.02	28.30		7
3.	DAVE NEWMAN				
4.	ANDY HALLIDAY	9.04	23.09		1
5.	DOMINIC BOND				
6.	JOSH TROTTER	9.06	26.52		6
7.	MALCOLM WOOLSEY				
8.	IAN McNALLY	9.08	23.36		2
9.	FRANK BOLD				
10.	ROLY COLLICOTT	9.10	25.18		4
11.	SHANE TOWNSEND				
12.	VINCE DEY	9.12	26.41		5
13.	JOHN SULLIVAN				
14.	PETER DIXON (WILLESDEN CC)	9.14	24.53		3
15.					
16.					
17.					
18.					
19.					
20.					

Early morning club TT result board.

Typical club rider TT position.

An evening time trial.

the 2011 Tour de France, won by Cadel Evans, was decided in the last time trial stage.

Position

An aerodynamic position that suits one rider may not suit another. One rider may be more flexible and can easily accommodate a large drop between saddle height and handlebar height, while another rider may need the handlebars raised by several centimetres.

Measurements such as limb and torso length will affect a rider's position and because of these variations there is no set formula to optimize a rider's position. Females generally have shorter torsos and longer legs than men. In addition, females may suffer more discomfort in extreme aerodynamic positions where their hips are rotated, as the saddle may put more pressure on the groin. These factors have to be taken into account when setting a position.

Before any position can be set, ensure the frame is the correct size for the purpose.

Generally time trial bike frames are smaller than normal road frames, so the distance between saddle height and handlebar height is greater. Also, time trial frames tend to have a seat tube angle of around 75 degrees, compared to 72–73 degrees for normal road frames. Having a steeper seat tube angle allows the rider to sustain a higher power output over relatively short durations and effectively rotates the rider forward, increasing the torso to lower-body angle and reducing the rider's frontal surface area.

Before trying to position the rider in an aerodynamic position, I always set the saddle height. When the rider's leg is in the bottom of the pedal stroke position – not necessarily the 6 o'clock position – the angle of the knee joint should be at 155 degrees. Once this has been set then you can go onto the other aspects. There are three points on the body that are the fulcrum points: the greater trochanter (bony protrusion of the hip), bony protrusion of the outside of the knee, and finally the maleolus (bony protrusion of the ankle).

I ran a TT positioning evening at my cycling club, measuring up a variety of riders. I showed them the ultimate position, as used by Britain's most successful rider, Bradley Wiggins.

This was the benchmark, as I believe it is the most aerodynamic and offers the most powerful riding position and therefore the fastest, which after all is the whole aim of the thing. This rider has a completely flat back and the elbows are almost at 90 degrees to his torso. Many riders naturally had varied positions. I made a wooden model with hinged joints to demonstrate how angles alter the body shape, and this turned out to be a good visionary tool.

The optimum angle for a rider to adopt in a time trial position is 1 degree above the horizontal. Many riders find it too difficult to achieve a position so close to the horizontal as it may be painful, and compromises breathing and work rate. This is particularly the case with untrained riders unaccustomed to a low

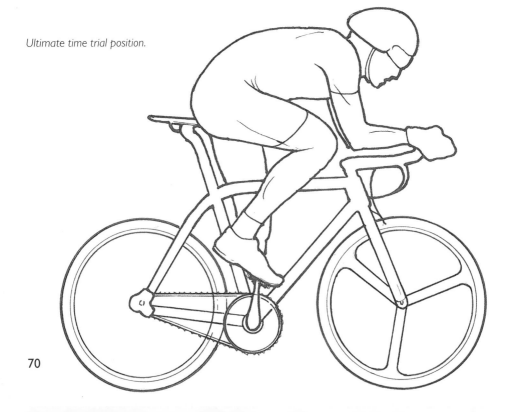

Ultimate time trial position.

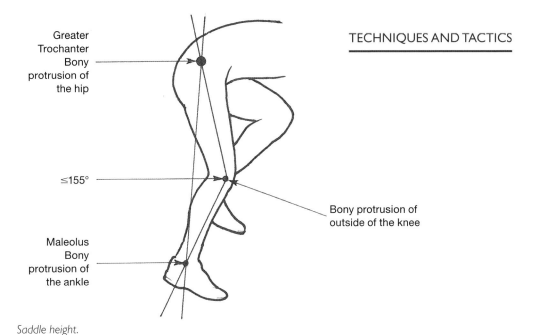

Greater Trochanter
Bony protrusion of the hip

≤155°

Maleolus
Bony protrusion of the ankle

Bony protrusion of outside of the knee

Saddle height.

position, as it takes time to adapt. You may find that you have to increase the angle to achieve relative comfort. It is much better to adopt a more upright position that you can maintain throughout the race than a more extreme position that you can't: although the latter may be more aerodynamic, if you are constantly stretching your back and getting out of this position, any benefits will be lost.

The angle of the upper arm should be close to 90 degrees with shoulders above the elbows. Any angle greater than 100 degrees shifts the rider's weight back on the saddle, which may result in discomfort and possibly saddle injuries.

With tri-bar arm rests, the width generally allows the arms to be in line with the thighs. Although many riders use flat bar extensions,

Upper arm angle.

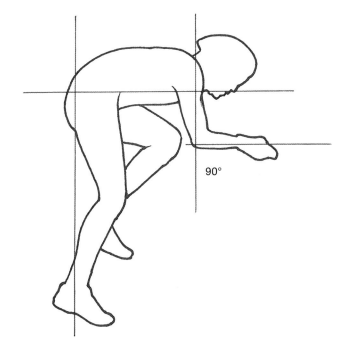

90°

*Time trial position
of club rider.*

this puts the wrists in a position beyond the normal range of movement; S-bend extensions, with a slight upwards bend from the horizontal, allow the wrists to sit in a more natural, comfortable position.

Your head should have a clear view of the road ahead for obvious safety reasons, and your eyes should be facing forwards, not looking down at the road. This position is actually more aerodynamic, especially when wearing an aerodynamic helmet. The ideal position is when the tip of the rear of the helmet touches the top of your back, resulting in less disruption to the airflow over you.

It is possible to convert a standard road bike to a time trial bike by fixing clip-on tri-bars to drop handlebars and by moving the saddle forward. Whatever you do, there will always be a compromise, as the frame will be designed to be ridden in a conventional position. The 72- to 73-degree seat tube angle makes it difficult to achieve the torso to horizontal position without making it too acute. The saddle can be positioned further forward but this reduces the saddle to handlebar reach so that it is too short and you are hunched over the bike. The best compromise is to develop a less extreme position that is relatively aerodynamic and allows you to handle the bike safely.

Time trial position for a rider shown on a road bike in a winter training workshop.

In summary:

- Adopt a flat back, or as flat as possible, taking into account how flexible you are. Most importantly, make sure you can maintain the position for the race duration. There's no point in constantly 'getting up' out of the position, disturbing the airflow.
- Ensure your elbows are inboard of your hips in the frontal position.
- Wear a skinsuit – undoubtedly the best TT clothing purchase you will ever make. Other pieces of clothing, including the right helmet, socks and shoes will help, but none as much as a skinsuit.
- If you can afford a bespoke TT bike with steeper frame angles, lower front end and the accessories described above then this is the ideal solution as it allows you to adopt the flat back position.

Stack and Reach

With some frame sizes, for example compact frames, two measurements become very important. These are stack and reach, and they are very useful for comparing different-sized frames reliably.

Stack is the vertical distance from the centre line of the bottom bracket to the top centre of the head tube.

Reach is the horizontal distance between the centre line of the bottom bracket to the centre of the head tube.

Both measurements are independent of the seat tube angle and do not change if you are using an integrated headset, so you can use them to replicate your position on frames of different sizes. A word of warning, however: bikes are designed to be ridden with the saddle and stem length fore/aft within a small range, and moving out of this range may compromise bike handling.

Short-Distance Time Trials

You have to maintain a high level of intensity of effort, which requires focus, concentration and motivation. Many riders lose their concentration, resulting in loss of speed. The shorter the distance, the more significant is

Short distance time trialist in action, showing maximum aerodynamic savings.

the loss of speed. If you miss out on an under-the-hour 25-mile ride by a handful of seconds you can see the consequences of this effect.

With an aerodynamic position you should be at your maximum speed throughout the race – that is, at a speed just below your threshold pace. Threshold (commonly referred to as lactate threshold) is the speed at which your

Tri-bars fitted to time trial bike.

body fails to keep up with the rate of lactate production. Excessive blood lactate combines to interfere with efficient and proper muscle contraction, with the result that you slow down. Being able to ride just below this level of effort so that lactate is constantly removed is the key. Sometimes you will go anaerobic – work above lactate threshold, for example by going uphill until the gradient slackens – but for the majority of the time you will ride just under the lactate threshold.

This is easier said than done, but riders new to this discipline must practise this skill if they want to be successful in this branch of the sport. Turbo training, especially in the winter, is ideal. Concentration, cadence (speed of pedalling) and holding a racing position are also imperative.

Therefore, training, especially for short-distance events, typically in the UK 10, 25 and 50 miles, is geared towards this. The UK also has hilly events, mainly early in the season and the season-long Rudy Project series held on technical hillier courses. The principles are the same, but on hilly courses and technical

Roundabout turn, early morning time trial with race marshals in position, gloves on showing the cold.

circuits bike handling ability is more crucial and riders have to be much more confident of their descending skills and cornering. Time trial bikes don't handle as well as conventional road bikes, and riders also have to make decisions about when and where to use tri-bars and when to get out of the saddle or stay seated.

On a 10-mile time trial, it is common for the rider to go off too quickly, and consequently fatigue prematurely. Top riders build up speed in the first mile, so after this they are at race speed, heart rate and power are both steady and a constant effort is being poured out. This effort is maintained for virtually the entire race. Only in the last 1–1.5 miles is the effort increased so the rider is at their 'limit' and crosses the line satisfied they have put in out as much effort as they possibly could.

It takes skill to ride in this manner and lots of practice. Practising this skill in the aerodynamic position is very effective. Refining your time trial start is also important. This can be practised in events you may designate as test events, for example mid-week races. Try different starts – going off too quick, starting slower, steadier – and see what suits you best, with hopefully an improvement in times. Once you've decided your tactics you know exactly what to do on race day so everything is far more settled, allowing you to concentrate on the race.

Generally, riders 'turn' on the course at roundabouts. Selecting the correct line and speed is therefore essential. Too many riders come into the roundabout too fast and brake on the bend, sometimes causing the rear wheel to skid. It is much better to brake beforehand, change gear if necessary, take the roundabout at a sensible speed without braking and then ratchet up the power on exit. This is by far the quickest method.

Normally riders don't use a bottle on 10- and 25-mile time trials, although in certain cases, such as hot summer days, it's a good idea. Generally, in 50-mile TTs a bottle is taken.

Early morning TT riders getting ready.

Long-Distance Time Trials

Riders need excellent aerobic endurance to be able to ride at speed for the longer time trials – 100 miles to 24 hours. Long hours are needed in the saddle to build up a large aerobic base and regular long rides are necessary to then get used to long periods in the saddle. Many riders find simply riding for long periods boring and physically difficult, never mind the intensity of the effort. Having a strong core and being flexible will improve comfort and performance as well.

A 100-mile race typically lasts between about 3.5 hours to over 5 hours, while distances covered in 12 hours range from between sub-200 miles to over 300 miles. On a 24-hour course the range is even greater, from sub-300 to over 500 miles, and this event is even more demanding with sleep deprivation to cope with as well.

Dehydration and glycogen depletion are massive causes of fatigue in these time trials and riders have to consume food and drink during these events. Riders must therefore carry both food and drink with them, in addition to what is offered to them by either their helpers or race officials. Although energy drinks have made great strides in recent years there are still many cases of riders suffering from gastro discomfort relying too heavily on gels and energy drinks alone. When riding

longer events many riders prefer solid food and water in order to remain hydrated or, at the very least, not dehydrated.

Technical demands for longer events are very similar to those of 25- and 50-mile time trials. However, the more extreme positions used in shorter events are replaced with a more comfortable, less aerodynamic position. Training in this position for long periods of time is recommended to get used to the demands of the event and to give the rider opportunities to experiment with their position and get it right for the event. Taking food and drink whilst on the move from a roadside helper should be practised, as should eating and drinking on the move.

The length of these events imposes many psychological demands on the rider. During the event riders will face their demons, so to speak, and experience both fatigue and discomfort, which will impact on their concentration. It is important to have strategies to overcome this, for example positive self talk and encouragement from coaches and helpers to motivate the rider.

An experienced support crew will work wonders for the rider; the crew's ability to deal with mishaps such as punctures and mechanical problems and keep the rider nutritionally satisfied and up to speed with race strategies is a godsend.

CHAPTER 4

Healthy Eating and Drinking

The importance of 'fuelling up' properly is not to be underestimated. This book cannot provide detailed information on nutrition and hydration but can provide guidelines on how healthy eating can aid performance, which after all is what we are seeking. A healthy diet for an active cyclist should revolve around energy derivation and include the three principal components of food:

- Rich carbohydrates
- Vegetable fat
- Moderate protein.

Whilst there are numerous magazines, books and websites that can provide sound dietary advice for the average person, the diet of a racing cyclist is different, requiring more carbohydrates. Special dietary require-ments, for example vegetarianism, will add complications but should not hinder performance providing adequate nutrition is provided.

Broadly speaking, people are advised to derive about half their daily calories from carbohydrates, including five portions of fruit and vegetables, and about a third from

Use the 'eatwell plate' to help you get the balance right. It shows how much of what you eat should come from each food group. © Department of Health in association with the Welsh Assembly Government, the Scottish Government and the Food Standards Agency in Northern Ireland

proteins (dairy, meat, fish), with the remainder coming from fats and oils.

The Food Standards Agency has produced the 'eatwell plate', which shows how much of what you eat should come from each food group. This includes everything you eat during the day, including snacks.

So, try to eat:

- Plenty of fruit and vegetables
- Plenty of bread, rice, potatoes, pasta and other starchy foods – choose wholegrain varieties whenever you can
- Some milk and dairy foods
- Some meat, fish, eggs, beans and other non-dairy sources of protein
- Just a small amount of foods and drinks high in fat and/or sugar.

Suggested proportions of the main food groups for cyclists:

- Carbohydrates 60–70 per cent
- Fats 20–25 per cent
- Protein 10–15 per cent.

Carbohydrates

Carbohydrate is an important fuel for cycling. To get an idea on the amount needed, an active cyclist training regularly will need about 7g of carbohydrate per day for every kilogramme of their body weight.

Our bodies break carbohydrates down into sugar and then burn the sugar as fuel for our brain and body. Your body must have a steady supply of glucose, the form of sugar that it breaks carbohydrates down to.

Complex carbohydrates are the 'good carbs'. These include whole grains, starchy vegetables and beans. They have complicated molecules that break down slowly, delivering a steady supply of sugar to the bloodstream.

When sugar is delivered to the cells gradually, they can burn it for energy and our energy levels stay stable.

The Glycaemic Index (GI) measures how fast and how much a food raises blood glucose levels. Food with higher index values raise blood sugar more rapidly than foods with lower GI values.

Simple carbohydrates with a high GI index are made of simple molecules that are easy for your body to break down and deliver sugar to the bloodstream quickly; 'bad carbs', such as sugary foods and foods made with white flour, fall into this category. These carbohydrates break down quickly and cause a spike in blood sugar levels: you will experience a rush of energy after eating them, then a big drop.

Not all simple carbohydrates are 'bad' though. Some, like fruit, are simple, nutritious carbohydrates. Fresh fruit gives us enzymes, vitamins, minerals and fibre. Milk products also offer important nutritional benefits like protein.

Before going out training, it's best to eat foods with low to moderate GI value 2–3 hours before exercise. If your training session lasts more than 60 minutes, top up with higher GI foods, for example bananas or energy bars/gels.

After you have completed your training, it's essential to eat/drink fairly quickly – within 20 minutes. After exercise nutrients from food and drink are absorbed by the liver and muscles, aiding quick recovery. A good snack would be a banana, jam sandwich or chocolate milkshake.

Complex carbohydrates are like good logs on a campfire, they burn steadily for a long time. The bad, simple carbohydrates are like dry twigs, they catch fire easily, flare up quickly and fizzle out. The table below gives examples of the different kinds of carbohydrates and when it's best to eat them.

GI Values of Different Foods

High GI		Moderate GI		Low GI	
Glucose	100	Croissant	67	Kidney beans (canned)	52
Sports drink	95	Couscous	65	Low-fat ice cream	50
Instant rice	91	Mars bar	65	Raw carrots	49
Honey	87	Raisins	64	Porridge	49
Cornflakes	80	Ryvita	63	Coconut	45
French fries	75	Boiled potato	62	Custard	43
Bagel	72	Hamburger bun	61	Apricot	43
		Blueberry muffin	59	Orange	43
		Baked potato	59	Strawberries	40
		Banana (ripe)	53	Milk	31
				Prunes	29

Time to eat	GI index	Example
Before training	Low/ moderate	Porridge Fruit – apple, orange, plum, peach Dried fruit – prunes, apricots Cereal – All Bran, muesli Milk – skimmed, low fat
During training	High	Energy gels Sports drinks Jaffa Cakes
After training	High	Sports drinks
Immediately after		Cornflakes Bagel, bananas
After training	Low/ moderate	Cereal, Weetabix
1–2 hours after		Wholemeal bread Potatoes Rice

Fats

Fat is a necessary part of a sports diet and comprises 15–30 per cent of calorie intake. Too much fat in a diet, however, will reduce the availability of carbohydrate by slowing the breakdown.

If you increase your carbohydrate consumption but do not reduce your fat intake, you will simply gain weight. Don't reduce fat too much, however, as there is evidence to show that too low fat a diet may be linked to heart disease and cancers.

Monounsaturated fats are probably the most beneficial fats for both sports performance and health. Good sources are oils, olive oil, rapeseed, almonds, hazelnuts and olives themselves.

Saturated fats have no positive benefits for either sports or health. Sources are from animal products – cheese, butter, lard and meat fat. Processed foods, such as cakes and biscuits, often contain large quantities of saturated fat as well, so are best avoided.

Polyunsaturated fats, found in most vegetable oils and oily fish such as mackerel, can reduce cholesterol levels in the blood. They also include essential fatty acids that the body can't make by itself and can only come from food. This type of fat is needed in moderation.

Protein

Active people require a higher intake of protein compared to sedentary people. Protein is needed to regenerate muscle tissue and maintain healthy bones. Proteins are formed from amino acids, and of the twenty types of amino acids needed, nine cannot be synthesized by the body. These have to be supplied regularly from the diet and are described as essential amino acids. Protein contains a wide range of amino acids and it is important that riders try to eat a good selection of protein-rich food, and this is even more important for vegetarians. Meat is an excellent provider of amino acids but also contains a high percentage of fat, so select the leanest cuts. Poultry and fish are recommended as both are lower in fat than red meat.

Aim to derive 12–15 per cent of your calories from protein.

Cycling Foods

In long races being able to eat on the move is essential, so selecting the correct food to prevent you running out of energy is vital. Eating correctly before and after the event/training ride is also crucial.

Eating little and often is ideal – when you feel hungry it's often too late. Popular snacks to take on the move are bananas, malt loaf wrapped in foil, raisins and cakes, while on a cold winter's ride a café stop might see beans on toast consumed with lots of tea.

Many riders find these foods easy to digest and they contain a good range of both simple and complex carbohydrates. Watch out with the tea though as it is diuretic and your mates won't thank you too much if you have to stop regularly to relieve yourself.

Chocolate bars are popular and provide a welcome energy boost, but they have a high sugar content, so if eaten on their own may cause a sugar rush that depletes the muscle glycogen stores. It's best to eat chocolate with other foods to mitigate this effect.

Here is an example of a nutrition strategy for a typical event, a 100-mile ride.

The day before the event, make sure you keep well hydrated and eat plenty of carbohydrates. Cut back on fats and eat more lean protein. Avoid curry and similar spicy dishes, which are liable to cause gastric upsets.

On the morning of the ride, rise early so that you leave plenty of time to consume a proper breakfast and let this settle. Both carbohydrate and protein are important dietary needs. Porridge with honey is a good option, as is a bagel with peanut butter and a banana. Avoid fibrous foods for obvious reasons! Ensure you start drinking plenty of fluids.

During the ride, start your nutrition early. What you eat in the first hour fuels you for the second, third and so on; don't wait until you feel hungry. Nibble on an energy bar and drink regularly (take two bottles). Good-quality sports drinks are ideal, together with plain water, as this does not upset the stomach.

After the ride, you may arrive back exhausted or euphoric, depending on how it went. When you finish, glug down a recovery drink straight away. Although you may not feel like consuming food, eat something in the first 20 minutes after completion, such as toast and jam, a peanut butter sandwich – something easily consumed. After washing, you'll feel like eating your regular meal. Again, don't forget your hydration.

Performance Drinking

When you exercise you produce heat. Sweat forms on the skin and evaporates, regulating your body temperature. Unless you replace this sweat loss by drinking you quickly dehydrate. Dehydration can be serious, ranging from life-threatening to irritation – it can cause headaches, for example. Even mild dehydration impairs sports performance.

Sweat tastes salty, a clear indication that you are losing minerals as well as water. There are many brands of electrolyte drinks on the market that offer to replace lost minerals. There is substantial benefit from these drinks but actual fluid loss is far greater than mineral loss whilst on the move so the important thing is to take in water. After exercise or on long rides this type of drink offers far greater benefit for topping up the body micronutrients.

Adopting a good drinking strategy in your lifestyle will pay dividends. In order to train/race well it is essential you are properly hydrated, so you should get used to drinking regularly throughout your normal day.

The NHS recommends drinking about 1.2 litres of fluid every day to prevent us from becoming dehydrated. This equates to six 200ml or eight 150ml glasses or 2.25 pints. This is the normal recommended intake for all adults, and of course for active cyclists it will be a great deal more. For example, in racing/training in hot conditions, an 80kg rider should aim to consume 700ml per hour.

The fluids referred to here include all non-alcoholic drinks, but water, milk and fruit juices are healthiest. Try to avoid fizzy and sugary drinks, which may be high in added sugars, high in calories and bad for your teeth.

Without doubt water is the healthiest choice for quenching your thirst at any time; it contains no calories or sugars that damage your teeth. Milk is a good source of calcium, a mineral that helps build and preserve healthy bones. Choose semi-skimmed, 1 per cent fat or skimmed milk. Fruit juice is first-rate, but carefully check the label and choose 100 per cent juice (not a fruit 'drink') with no added sugar. Importantly this also counts as one of your 'five per day'.

Tea and coffee both contain caffeine, which is a stimulant, so can make you temporarily feel alert or drowsier. This of course depends on how much you consume. Whilst it is fine to drink tea and coffee as part of your diet they produce more urine. Energy drinks often contain high levels of caffeine and many are high in sugars and sometimes other stimulants, such as vitamins, minerals or herbal substances. Although caffeine levels in these drinks vary, in many cases there is 80mg of caffeine in a small 250ml can, which is about the same as two cans of cola or a small mug of coffee.

For most of us training/racing for less than 60 minutes, a combination of water and diluted squash is perfectly fine. Aim to drink 500–750ml to compensate for dehydration.

For events/training longer than 60 minutes, consider an isotonic sports drink. This type of drink contains a small amount of carbohydrate to boost energy levels.

Although you may read many promotional articles that extol the benefits of energy drinks treat them with a little scepticism. One promotional tool used is advertising the amount of carbohydrate they contain. Bear in mind if the content is too high, the body won't be able to remove the fluid from the stomach and into the bloodstream where it is necessary.

Isotonic drinks, on the other hand, have carbohydrate levels of about 5–8 per cent, or, if you prefer, 5–8g per 100ml of fluid. This amount does not hinder the absorption of the fluid and imparts a little extra energy. There is also a small amount of sodium (salt) to aid the absorption as well. The big benefit of an isotonic drink is that it is a good all-rounder and can be used before, during and after training/racing.

You can make your own isotonic drinks with the following recipes:

- Make up 1 litre of fruit squash diluted with four to five parts water and add 1/5 of a teaspoon of salt.
- Make up 1 litre diluted squash with 60g of glucose or sugar and add 1/5 of a teaspoon of salt.
- As above, but instead of the glucose or sugar, use 100g glucose polymer powder, sometimes called maltodextrin.
- Pure fruit juice diluted 50:50 with water with 1/5 of a teaspoon of salt per litre.

A word of warning: be careful with your teeth with any type of commercial sports drink. Many have a pH of 5.5 or below, which means it is acidic (commercial water has a pH value between 6 and 8.5). Values of 5.5 and below can damage the enamel on the outside of your teeth. To minimize this effect sports drinks should be taken cold, and don't swish the liquid around your mouth but swallow it quickly. Consume by the mouthful, don't drink in small sips. And, of course, clean your teeth regularly.

Alcohol

The British Dietetic Association (BDA) states that moderate consumption of alcohol has been shown to have a protective effect against coronary heart disease amongst men and women, especially women over fifty or post-menopausal. Red wine in particular contains beneficial substances that may protect artery walls. Experts recommend one to two glasses per day. If you drink more than this amount, the potential detrimental effects, such as liver cirrhosis, are greater than any positive effects. Have at least two alcohol-free days per week.

About 20 per cent of alcohol is absorbed into the bloodstream through the stomach and the remainder through the small intestine. The liver breaks down most of the alcohol, but it can only break alcohol down at a fixed rate of approximately one unit per hour. Any alcohol consumed above this limit is dealt with by a different enzyme system (MEz) in the liver to make it less toxic to the body. Drinking more alcohol means more MEz enzymes are produced, which is why you can develop an increased tolerance to alcohol. However, drinking too much can cause hangovers, headaches, thirst, nausea, vomiting and heartburn, so keep it under control.

Summary

There is an enormous amount of information on food and various diets now available. Much of it is good but a great deal is misleading and confusing. Just remember that the basic guidelines are fairly obvious and haven't changed for decades. Eat a good, basic, balanced diet containing with plenty of fresh fruit and vegetables.

Avoid processed and fatty foods. Carbohydrate should be your staple food, with protein and fat in the correct measures making up the rest of your diet. Keeping well hydrated is essential. Avoid excess of anything, though the occasional blow-out or big fry-up won't do you any harm – remember, this is your hobby, not your profession.

Many excellent articles on diets can be found in various magazines, such as *Cycling Weekly*; both the BDA and NHS websites provide valuable information as well. If you want to delve deeper into this subject then Anita Bean's book *The Complete Guide to Sports Nutrition* is excellent and regarded as the ultimate read in this subject.

Seek out a qualified dietician if you need a tailor-made diet, ideally a member of the BDA.

CHAPTER 5

Looking After Yourself

Appearance

If you go to a local race and look at the regular winners, you will notice they are generally well turned out with immaculate bikes. Attention to these details, in training as well as racing, makes for good performances as well as creating a good impression.

It costs nothing to keep yourself and your bike clean. You may not have the best equipment in the world but if it is clean and well maintained that counts for a lot more than dirty, ill-maintained equipment. Problems like frayed brake cables, tyre cuts or even cracked frames are easily spotted in regular maintenance. This is more important now then ever

An immaculate bike, checked and ready to race.

Handlebar tape expertly wound on.

before with the popularity of carbon, because, unlike metal, which gives a warning, carbon simply fails, with catastrophic consequences.

If you can afford it and don't want the bother, why not take your bike for a service at the end of each season? That way, at the start of each season you are safe in the knowledge that you've covered this base.

You often hear of riders puncturing in races, and there are genuine cases, but sometimes you look at the tyres and wonder how on earth they got as far as they did.

A pet hate of mine is scruffy handlebar tape. Having held up many riders in time trials over the years, I've noticed that handle-bars are often cluttered up with all sorts of gadgets, computers, heart rate monitors and power meters, clamped at various angles on the most dirty, fraying handlebar tape. Riders frequently wipe their noses with bare hands then transfer their hands to the handlebars (complete with offending mucus), where germs multiply. The tape is never changed although this is cheap compared to the assortment of ancillaries that are frequently fitted. Ensure it is changed regularly.

Handlebar set-up with immaculate bar tape and Garmin mounted on stem.

Keeping Healthy

Hygiene

Keep clean Wash shorts regularly to avoid saddle sores, which can wreck your season – or, in the case of one professional, his career, as the sore never healed and he had to pack in cycling. Normally saddle sores are the result of a poor position and dirty clothing. Ensure all your training gear is washed regularly, to kill bacteria and avoid embarrassing skin problems. Be careful with biological powders; they need to be well rinsed or certain skin complaints could arise.

Upon returning back from a training run, have a wash as quickly as possible, then change into clean clothes. Don't hang around in damp clothing.

Hands Ensure you have clean fingernails – preferably short, although this may be more difficult for lady riders. If you scratch your skin with dirty nails you are tempting skin problems. Regular hand washing during your normal day will eliminate the majority of bacteria that we pick up and could cause infections. Racing mitts and gloves are a source of infection, especially when they are used to wipe your nose, so, like shorts, wash them regularly.

Feet These take a great deal of punishment so it's worth taking care of them. Cut toenails straight across, not rounded at the corners, or you risk in-growing toenails. With the advent of clipless pedals, I've noticed some riders experience hard patches of skin at the pressure point. Unlike the old toe-clip design, where the pressure point was more evenly distributed along the pedal, the modern pedal has a far more focused spot. Keep an eye on this as hard skin builds up and can become quite painful. In some cases a visit to the chiropodist may be necessary.

Head Always wear a well-fitting helmet on all rides. Countless articles have been written on

Cork ribbon handlebar tape.

Cycle racing mitts.

Race drinking bottle firmly mounted on the bike.

the pros and cons of this particular piece of equipment. Having attended and competed in many races I have been amazed in certain cases how riders have picked themselves off the road after a crash with a shattered helmet only to look dazed. Without this piece of polystyrene protecting their skull, heaven knows what would have happened.

Clothing With the event of modern fabrics, cyclists' lives have never been so good. Modern undervests dissipate moisture away from the skin, keeping you relatively dry. On cold, windy days, it's worth taking a windproof top and tucking this into one of your spare pockets.

Drinking bottles One horror story I read once was to do with drinking bottles. On a wet, cold ride during the winter months a rider regularly drank from his bottle. His front wheel sprayed up road water onto the mouth piece. Unbeknownst to him, the road water contained contaminants that cause Weil's disease (from rats' urine), and this

Good example of drinking on the move in a race while expertly keeping the bike under control.

contaminant entered his body via the teat of the drinking bottle. He suffered from a fever for a few days, but this is a serious infection and may spread to the brain, liver, kidneys and heart, and has a 10 per cent mortality rate. Some drinking bottles now have a cover over the teat protecting this area, which is well worth investing in, especially for the wet winter months.

Make sure your bottle is washed regularly after every ride. For those of you who have a dishwasher, use it, as this equipment is very effective. Most bottles these days are dishwasher proof, but check first. If you don't have access to a dishwasher, then soak well and scrub.

Overtraining and Tiredness

A top European cyclist once recommended, 'Don't stand when you can sit down, and don't sit down when you can lie down'. Most of us in the normal world do not have this luxury, but there is a serious point here.

Rest is important, so work at it. Getting a good night's sleep is essential. Many individuals only need six hours but others may need eight or nine. Try this simple experiment. When you are not racing and there are no other important functions going on, go to bed at your normal time and sleep until you naturally wake up. Try doing this for a period of over a week and you will be able to calculate your natural sleeping need. If you then need to get up at a particular time, for example to go to work, you can adjust your bedtime accordingly to ensure you sleep for the correct amount of time.

If you are feeling very weary, unaccountably so, you may be overtrained. Bear in mind you may be overtrained even on six hours' training per week at high intensity with little or no rest, so this condition is not limited to high performers. Of course you should be tired from training but after a good night's sleep recovery should almost be complete, in most cases overnight and certainly during the next day. Taking your pulse first thing in the morning is a clear indication of your condition. If it is ten beats or more higher than normal this points to overtraining.

This is a tricky situation, as to go fast you need to train hard and recover, then train hard, recover again. The more you train, the more your fitness improves and the faster you recover. Other situations may interfere though. For example, imminent redundancy, financial worries, a new baby, moving home are all factors that remove a chunk from your energy reserves and put you under stress.

Training too hard and too long coupled with any of the above factors can leave you exhausted and fatigue sets in. Sleep patterns are affected and all you want to do is collapse in a chair.

In a case like this, cease training normally, rest and see your doctor to rule out any possible medical problems. Once you've been given a clean bill of health, seek to regain your normal balance.

Eat and drink well and get as much rest as you can. For the time being avoid activities connected with cycling, and try concentrating on different ones instead. Should you wish to train, then simply train fartlek (unstructured interval training). Don't analyse your activities in any detail, simply enjoy what you are doing. If you have a coach, discuss your problems and formulate a recovery plan. It may be that you have to stop training/racing for a period of time.

Injuries

Normally injuries to knees are the result of overuse, although they can also be the result of a crash or in certain cases old, sporting injuries picked up from another sport that has manifested itself through cycling.

The most common causes of knee pain related to cycling are:

- Incorrect saddle height
- Incorrect cleat adjustment
- Overuse of big gears
- Damaged equipment, especially bent pedal spindles
- Physical differences – for example, one leg longer than the other.

Consult an expert if problems persist, as there are many remedies on the market now that were unheard of years ago.

Crashes

As someone once told me, there is one sure thing if you cycle: at some point you will fall off. Not very reassuring, but true. Perhaps strangely, serious injuries are rare although most involve road rash, which is very painful.

Seek a doctor's opinion immediately, however. It has not been uncommon for cyclists to be wandering around after a crash for weeks, only to discover that that dull aching wrist is in fact broken and could have been put in plaster weeks ago, thus salvaging a season instead of wrecking it.

It is well worth having a tetanus jab, as you can easily pick up infections from road rash or indeed from insect bites, which are more prevalent in the summer months, or, less commonly, animal bites.

RICE is a very effective way to deal with minor injury traumas on soft tissue.

R is for **rest** and prevents further damage.
I is for **ice** – application of an ice pack (special packs can be purchased) will reduce bleeding from damaged blood vessels by making them contract, and reduce possible bruising.
C is for **compression**, usually in the form of a pressure bandage to control swelling.
E is for **elevation** – lifting the injured limb above the heart level reduces excessive blood flow to the injury. This will help to

reduce the pressure of fluid on the injured limb and keeps bruising to a minimum.

Following these four instructions quickly will enable the healing process to begin.

Stretching

It is sometimes difficult to persuade cyclists to stretch on a regular basis. However, the benefits are immense, as stretching:

- Reduces muscle soreness following training/racing
- Reduces muscle tension
- Reduces the likelihood of back problems
- Assists in the repair phase following injury
- Stimulates the production of lubricating fluid in the joints, helping to reduce adhesion between tissue and mitigating the aging effects on joints
- Ensures muscles are at optimal working length
- Improves circulation
- Develops body awareness, allowing for a more holistic approach to injury prevention and recovery.

Static Stretching

There are three main types of stretching: static, dynamic and PNF. Static is the one we should be most concerned with. It can be performed more easily, is safer and is very effective. Static stretching involves slowly and carefully stretching a muscle to the end of a range of movement or a point of tightness without causing discomfort, and then holding this for 15–30 seconds. Stretching should be performed on a regular basis about two or three times per week, and most certainly after a training ride or race, when the muscles will be warm and more receptive to stretching.

Stretching can help performance as long as stretches are performed correctly and are sport specific. It has been shown that after a period of ten weeks, a static stretching programme improved performance in tests involving speed, strength, power and endurance – all important characteristics for cyclists. Furthermore, greater flexibility will make you more comfortable on the bike so you will be able to work more effectively at higher intensities.

Stretching the back line–hip flexors and quads.

- Precede stretches with a warm-up to elevate muscle temperature.
- Stretch to the end of the range of movement or point of tightness without inducing discomfort.
- Hold each stretch for 15–30 seconds.
- Repeat each stretch two to four times.

Two of the most important aspects of a cyclist's anatomy are the back line and the front line. The back line is from the sole of your foot through the hamstrings, gluteal muscles and lower back muscles to your lower ribcage. The front line runs from the bottom of your rib-cage through your hip flexors and quadriceps to the knee.

Both back and front line are important as you need to achieve forward flexion at the hip and lower back. A cyclist with short hamstrings and gluteal muscles will not be able to achieve a low position on the bike and may experience problems ranging from pain in any back line muscle to loss of power. In time trialling in particular you need to be able to hold an aerodynamic position, and being flexible is important to help you achieve this.

Stretching Exercises

Below are some stretches that will help you achieve the correct range of motion, but remember to follow the stretching rules.

Quadriceps (front of thigh)

1. Hold your right foot with your right hand.
2. Bend the supporting (left) leg.
3. Push the pelvis forward to induce stretch in the middle of the muscle.
4. Repeat on the other side.

Hamstring group (back of thigh)

1. Extend the leg to be stretched.
2. Transfer your weight to the rear leg and bend knee.
3. Lift lower end of trunk up to lengthen spine.

Stretching quadriceps.

Stretching adductor – inner thigh.

Stretching hamstring group – back of thigh.

4. Keep head and shoulders up.
5. Avoid locking the knee and relax the foot.
6. Repeat with the other leg.

Adductor (inner thigh)

1. Feet should be shoulder width and a half apart.

2. Turn the left foot out and transfer your weight onto the left leg to stretch inside of the right thigh.
3. Keep your knee behind your toes. Widen stance if necessary.
4. Repeat on other side.

Back extension stretch

1. Lie face down and bring your hands up next to your shoulders.
2. Push up with your arms while arching backwards and looking up straight ahead.

Post-ride hamstring stretch

1. Lie down and extend your leg until you have a full stretch in the hamstring.
2. On every stretch, try and increase the range of the stretch.
3. Repeat on the other leg.

Back extension stretch.

Gastrocnemius (calf muscle/back of lower leg)

1. Stand with feet hip width apart.
2. Step back with one leg keeping feet hip width apart.
3. Press heels down, feet pointing forward.
4. Lean forward to keep spine and lower leg aligned. Use a chair/wall for support of the upper body.
5. Repeat with the other leg.

Post-ride stretch

This is actually a good stretch for both before and after riding.

1. Pull your knee to a 90-degree angle at the hip.
2. Hold your leg in this position through the full range of the stretch.
3. Repeat with the other leg.

Post-ride hamstring stretch.

Stretching gastrocnemius – calf muscles at back of lower leg.

After riding stretch 1.

Massage

There have been many articles on this subject, both for and against, but there seems to be very little scientific evidence on the matter. Recently (2011) there has been research carried out by Manchester University showing that physiological changes occur in the muscles during a massage and biochemical sensors are triggered that send inflammation-reducing signals to the muscle cells.

Furthermore, massage sends signals to the muscles to build more mitochondria, which are the power centres of cells and play an important role in healing.

Although this field is in its infancy, early results suggest that massage therapy blunts muscle pain by the same biological mechanisms as most pain medications and could be an effective alternative to them.

It is fair to say that after a massage many people feel great and their muscles are less sore. If you can manage to massage sore,

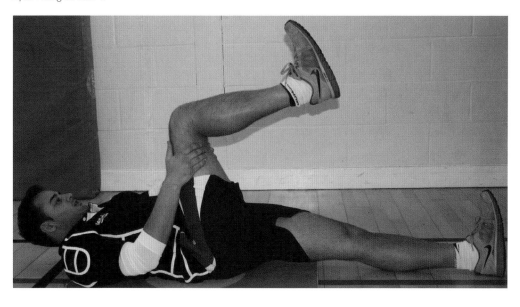

aching legs after a hard ride it will certainly relax you.

The following simple self-massage is well worth doing.

Warm-up Sit on a towel or on the edge of a bed or chair, make yourself comfortable and bend your knees. With your hands on the sides of your thighs, make quick up-and-down motions, loosening your upper-leg muscles as if you were brushing crumbs off your hands. Work your way down your leg, loosening your quadriceps, hamstring and calf. Switch legs after one minute.

After race/training ride Apply a few drops of massage oil – or olive oil at a pinch – to your upper thigh. Use your fingers to slowly knead your quads and hamstrings, moving upward from your knee. After a minute or two, reverse direction while applying more pressure. Repeat the process on your other thigh and your lower legs.

When not to massage Deep massage can irritate nerve endings, causing soreness, so avoid it the night before an event. Because your body diverts blood from the muscles to the stomach during digestion, it's not a good idea to have a massage straight after a meal either.

A good lubricant for self-massage is baby oil. It is designed for sensitive skin and unlikely to produce an adverse reaction. Just use enough to lubricate and eliminate painful friction from the palm of your hand, not so much that you can't grip with your hands.

Age

This section is especially relevant for veteran riders, who constantly amaze us all by pushing back the age barrier or so it seems. After the age of forty, it is a poignant fact that age and fitness seem to battle it out, and time eventually wins this battle. Be positive though – the benefits of taking regular exercise over a sedentary lifestyle are something to behold.

You read in cycling magazines the amazing times that veteran riders achieve, bettering the times they did in their twenties. For example, an eighty-year-old male competitor recently beat the hour for 25 miles, which is simply astonishing.

In physical terms the aging process can be summarized as follows:

20–35 years Biological and physical peak – it doesn't get any better.

35–45 years Physical activity usually declines and body fat starts to accumulate (about 5–10kg).

45–65 years Further decline in physical activity and as a result weight and fitness issues.

65–75 years Sometimes modest increase in activity as a result of retirement.

75–85 years Physical disability may develop.

As we age, our maximum heart rate decreases by about 5bpm per decade. Maximal oxygen uptake (VO_2max) decreases by about 10 per cent per decade. Joints and connective tissues are affected through dehydration, adhesions, changes in chemical structure, increased calcium deposits and changes in muscle fibre composition. Bone density can decrease, leaving us more prone to injury and other genetic factors, increase in fat and decrease in lean body tissue.

Cycle racing is an excellent aerobic activity for veterans. Although top-end speed may decline, for endurance events this is not so evident. Veteran riders may have more time on their hands – children grown up, possibly retired – but more is not necessarily best.

Endurance rides, going out on the café run, are probably more prevalent in this age group, to the detriment of intensity. There are many articles on endurance versus intensity that show not only should veteran riders continue with intensity sessions but should try to increase them. 'Use it or lose it' was never so pertinent, if veteran riders want to hold off lean tissue loss and maintain fast-twitch muscle firing at optimal levels.

With many years of endurance work in their legs a little exchange for intensity will do no harm, especially as races for veterans are generally shorter in distance.

Veteran riders find that it takes longer to gain form compared to younger rivals. Therefore, it is important to maintain a good level of base fitness and not let it slip too much. To get up to speed takes time after any lay-off – due to illness, holidays or injuries – so be patient.

Recovery is very important and should be treated as part of the training plan, and an afternoon nap on the sofa should not be frowned upon.

CHAPTER 6

Workout Plans and Race Preparation

The first part of this chapter provides a number of workout plans, both on the road and turbo, which covers most eventualities, and will ensure you are as ready as you can be for race day.

Before you start any of them, warm up for 10–30 minutes, depending on the activity, and after the workout cool down and then stretch the muscles for several minutes.

Aim to have a recovery drink after the effort.

Workout Plans

Endurance Workouts

E1 – Recovery 90rpm. Ride in small chain ring. Cadence 90, try to keep in Z1.

E2 – Endurance rolling. HR mainly in Z1/Z2. Try to remain in the saddle.

E3 – Endurance. Ride a rolling course in Z1/Z2, stay seated on hills. Ride a course and use gearing that allows work intensity into Z3.

Front of bike showing clean aerodynamic lines.

Time trial bike with modern groupset.

Skills and Speed Workouts

S1 – Spin step-ups. Ride on indoor trainer. Warm up with low resistance at cadence 90. After warm-up increase cadence to 100 for 3 minutes, 110 for 2 minutes and 120 for 1 minute. Spin easy to warm down.

S2 – Isolated leg. On trainer do 100 per cent of the work with one leg while the other is supported. Ride 1 minute one leg, 1 minute the other. Build up to maximum of six per leg.

S3 – Accelerations to work on leg speed. Warm up then complete the intended number of 30-second accelerations with 2.5-minute intervals between accelerations.

S4 – Fartlek. Ride mostly in Z1/2 with a few 10- to 20-second accelerations placed throughout the ride, spin easy between efforts.

S5 – Cadence. Ride in Z1/2 on a flat rolling course at cadence 90.

Hill workout

H1 – Hill climb. Find a hill that takes about 2–3 minutes to climb – one that is fairly steep but not too steep so that you can spend some time in the saddle and some time out of the saddle. Select a start and finish point, ride the hill as fast as you can using any style you prefer. Time yourself. Ride the prescribed number of intervals. After each interval turn around and

A mountain climb showing the great French cyclist Bernard Thevenet.

go back easy to the bottom and start next interval.

Muscular Endurance Workouts

M1 – Tempo. After warm-up ride at Z3 on a mostly flat course.

M2 – Z3. On a mostly flat course or indoor trainer complete the intervals prescribed, allowing your HR to rise into Z3 over the course of the interval. For example, do four or five sets of 4-minute rides, allowing HR to rise into Z3 and no higher. After HR is in Z3 try to hold it there until the end of the interval. Begin timing the interval as soon as you begin an increased effort. Spin easy for 60 seconds between efforts.

M2 – Z4/5. On a mostly flat course or indoor trainer complete the specified number of intervals, with 60 seconds easy spinning between efforts.

Speed Endurance (Anaerobic) Workouts

AA – Stretching exercises. See previous chapter. Duration 15–30 minutes.

A1a – Easy group ride. Ride with a group and stay mostly in Z1–3.

A1d – Ride as you feel. If you are feeling great, ride aggressively with some time in all zones.

A1c – Fast and aggressive group ride. Ride with a group riding in all zones but be aggressive and power up hills, chase riders who might have been faster than you in the past and have fun.

A2 – Speed endurance intervals. Warm up for 15–20 minutes. Ride a number of intervals allowing the heart rate to climb into Z5/Z6. The intervals may be ridden on the turbo or road slightly uphill. The idea of the interval is to raise your HR to Z5; start timing when the effort begins and end when effort ends. Take 3 minutes between each interval.

A7 – Taper intervals. Warm up, then complete the specified number of 90 accelerations, getting HR into Z4/Z5. Take 3 minutes to recover.

The open road – a flat stretch of road in the Chilterns.

Power Workouts

P1 – Sprints getting started. Warm up 15–20 minutes then complete a number of sprints and spin easy with low load between each sprint. For example, do five to seven sets of 10-second sprints, each building power throughout. Recover for 4 minutes 50 seconds between each sprint. Power or speed should be the same by the end of each sprint.

Test Workouts

T2 – Time Trial. Warm up for 15–20 minutes and then complete a 5- to 8-mile time trial as fast as you can possibly ride. The course

A two-up time trial with both competitors riding 'fixed'.

Bike set up on turbo in the shed.

needs to be clear of obstructions, traffic lights, stop junctions and similar obstacles. Use any gear you wish, change at will. Record conditions, wind, temperature, gears used, average heart rate, your current weight and how you felt out of 10. Repeat test in similar conditions as often as possible.

Turbo-Only Workouts

Before starting any turbo sessions, warm up thoroughly for 10–15 minutes, longer if you need to. Cool down after the session for 5–10 minutes pedalling easily.

If you can, it helps if you have a permanent set-up so you can just jump on the bike and are not put off by difficult turbo set-ups, fiddling with the adjustment screws, for example, and getting the correct roller pressure on the tyre.

Place a towel over the top tube as you will sweat a great deal, have a clock on the wall with a second hand and most importantly a fan, preferably 40cm in diameter, to keep you cool. Even on the coldest days in my shed – –10°C – I've been steaming away, but I have had to wear gloves as my hands got chilled initially holding the cold handlebars.

Mount your computer on the rear wheel so you know the speed you're riding at. A cadence sensor is a useful addition as well.

To spice things up, some riders watch specific cycling videos such as Sufferfest (www.thesufferfest.com/video-sufferfests), which take away the boredom of riding indoors.

Short Turbo Plans
These last 10–30 minutes only, so every minute counts. Don't be alarmed if you only have this amount of time, as the following

A turbo workout.

plans provide great training sessions. These sessions are about fitting in fitness around your lifestyle. It's about being time-savvy and not time-selfish. Some of these sessions may only last 20 minutes. But three extra 20-minute mini-rides per week add up to over 50 hours per year, so these sessions are not to be sniffed at. For many of us this is our bread and butter riding until the next oasis of a weekend where we can ride for 1–3 hours and bank this time.

Tabata repetitions A swift 23 minutes including warm-up and cool-down. Even the busiest of us can cram this session into their day. Ride six repetitions of 20 seconds at maximal intensity with only a 10-second rest between. Added up it only totals three gruelling minutes but the benefits are significant.

One-legged cycling Study the professionals and you'll notice how efficient their pedalling action is. This has taken years to develop. You can work on this yourself with one-legged cycling. Try riding two sets of 30 seconds left leg only, 30 seconds right leg only, high cadence both legs 5 minutes hard, 2 minutes easy; then two sets of 30 seconds left leg only, 30 seconds right leg only, high cadence 4 minutes hard.

Four! Four efforts of 4 minutes at the most you can ride in four minutes.

Fitness and fun Ride in alternate variations of 8 seconds fast sprint or 100rpm for 30 seconds. Ride this every 3 minutes.

Longer turbo plans
These are sessions lasting from 30 to 90 minutes.

Race pace repetitions Ride six sets of 3 minutes hard (race pace) with 3-minute rest between efforts. You can progress this by reducing the recovery by a minute or increasing the number of efforts.

Lactate threshold repetitions

Lactate threshold is the cycling intensity at which your legs start to hurt. However, it is one of the most important physiological factors that determine how hard you can ride and is caused by your body producing so much lactic acid that it interferes with your muscle fibres, causing pain and stiffness. Luckily, training around your intensity is an effective method of improving it. Repetitions should be progressive, so each month increase the speed/power or duration by around 5 per cent.

Thirty-Five Ride for 30 seconds at 120rpm, which will be 60 revs on a gear of about 53x16 at maximum heart rate. Note you will hit your max HR with about 10 or 5 seconds to go at Z6. Recover for 1 minute and repeat five times. Then ride for 5 minutes at your 10-mile time-trial pace.

Fifteen all Ride two sets of 15 minutes hard at a constant speed Z5, recovering between efforts with a 3-minute rest, pedalling gently.

Classic time trial intervals Ride for 5 minutes at an effort that can just be sustained for 5 minutes (Z5/Z6) – you will be hanging on at the end, desperate for the effort to finish. Recover for 5 minutes and go again. Aim to ride five time trial efforts in total. Your cadence should be maintained between 90 and 100rpm.

Fifteen over thirty Ride 15-second intervals at around 90 per cent of your maximum heart rate (MHR) Z5, spaced with 30 seconds' recovery intervals pedalling easily. In a 10-minute duration you will ride thirteen of these. Ride easily for 5 minutes and then ride another 10-minute set. If you're feeling fit then ride another set. Note the interval effort is not a sprint and the key is regular pacing so that you can repeat it at the same level all way through.

The stage is yours Stage 1 – ride for 15 minutes at 90–95rpm on gear size 53x16. Recover for 5 minutes' easy pedalling.

Stage 2 – ride for 10 minutes at 95–100rpm on a gear size 53x15. Recover for 5 minutes by riding easy.

Stage 3 – ride for 5 minutes as hard as possible at 100+ rpm Z5.

Three set match Ride for 5 minutes at Z4, followed by 2 minutes easy. Then do three sets of 2 minutes fast 105+ rpm Z5/Z6 with 30 seconds' recovery between efforts pedalling easily. Do 2 minutes easy riding. Ride six sets of 1 minute at 110+ rpm Z5/Z6 with 30-second recovery between efforts. Do another 2 minutes easy riding. Finish with eight sets of 30 seconds fast 110+ rpm Z5/Z6 with 30 seconds' recovery between efforts.

One minute at a time This exercise aims to simulate attacks in road races. Ride two sets of seven to ten 60-second efforts with a 1- or 2-minute recovery after each and 5 minutes of easy pedalling between sets. Ride as hard as you possibly can (Z5/Z6) but maintain consistency for the interval. For example, if you can hold 30mph for each interval but no more then this is the intensity you need to ride at. Over time, of course, as you get fitter this speed will increase.

Race Day Preparation

You've done the training: now focus on the matter in hand, which, after all, is the whole thing you are working for, the race.

For the few days before the race, make sure that you keep hydrated – your urine should be pale – and that you keep eating a carbohydrate-rich diet. It's normally easy to stay topped up since you'll also be reducing your training load.

A good night's sleep.

Deep section carbon front wheel.

Whatever your race, you should have a rehearsed preparation routine for both before and after the race, so that you can commence your recovery.

Preparation for the weekend's race should start at the beginning of the week. This may sound strange but the race will determine the training volume intensity of the preceding week, whether it is a big event or simply a training race where the process is much more important than the result.

For a start, if it is a big event, then you don't really want to be going out socializing and coming home late. In the real world the demands of our loved ones sometimes dictate what we are doing in other areas of our lives. We may have to attend a wedding reception, for example, which you will know about many weeks in advance. So in your wisdom you will not schedule an important race that takes two or three hours' travelling time to get to, requiring you to rise at the crack of dawn, for the day after the reception. You may simply want to race a local event that you can ride out to in less than an hour.

Clearly, planning is crucial. Purchase a planning sheet and write down the events you intend to race, starring the big races. Then insert the other events that you need to attend, such as weddings, parties, holidays and so on. There may be some need for compromise.

Once this in place you have a snapshot of the racing year, can plan more effectively and be confident mentally that you've covered all the bases. Of course, unexpected things crop up from time to time, like illness or work-related travel, but this is no excuse not to plan the things you do have control over: unless you plan, then you will simply plan to fail.

Road racing bike.

With your racing year planned, focus on your eating requirements prior to the race. The day before the race is the most important meal. You will be seeking energy food, so focus on carbohydrates – for example, pasta, potatoes and bread – and avoid alcohol. Eat early so you have digested the meal properly before going to bed.

Assuming you are racing on Sunday, a good night's sleep is far more important on Friday night than Saturday night. Many riders do not sleep well on nights before races. Rather than trying to force yourself to sleep well, it is far better to accept this and

focus on getting good-quality sleep on the previous night.

Preparing the Bike and Race Bag

Ensure the bike is checked over and leave nothing to chance. If you think a tyre needs changing because there are too many cuts in the tread, then change it. You may want to schedule an hour per week for this essential maintenance. The last thing you want is to travel to an event and puncture because you did not attend to this detail. It is a waste of your time, money and valuable energy.

Pack your race bag, assuming you are

Race bag partially packed for the event.

travelling to the race by car. Of course, if it is only a local club 10-mile time trial, your needs are going to be far simpler and can be contained in a back pocket.

The table below provides a comprehensive list of what you need to pack. It covers all eventualities and you may want to trim it down to suit your precise needs.

Event checklist

Holdall bag	General items	Equipment bag
House keys	Toothbrush/paste	Jerseys
Race instructions	Underwear	Shorts
Money	Extra clothes	Arm warmers
Sunglasses	Extra shoes	Leg warmers
Maps	Jumpers	Jacket
Music	T-shirts	Vest
Travel food	Tights (for ladies)	Socks
Camera	Jeans	Helmet
Mobile and charger	Shorts	Shoes – bike
Computer if necessary	Hat	Gloves
Suntan cream	Pyjamas	Sunglasses
	Long-sleeved shirt	
		Items for after the event:
		Towel
		Shower kit to include all paraphernalia
		First aid kit

Repairs	Food and drink	
Spare tubes Spare tyre Pump Chain lube Cleaning rags Tools Safety pins Cutters String Cable ties (assorted)	Energy drink Energy drink powder Gels Water Spare bottles Food of your choice	
Last-minute checks Water bottles full? Energy drink in the bottle? Gears set for the off? Tyres inflated?	Brakes centred – wheels spun? Chain lubricated? Race number on? Have you warmed up? Sunblock on? Helpers primed?	

Morning of the Race

For races that are shorter then an hour, it is far more important what you eat and drink beforehand than on the race day itself. This commences in training. Short-distance events, whether this is a time trial or 1-hour circuit race, demand you work right at your aerobic limits, especially for time trial.

If the event is in the morning, get up about 4 hours beforehand and have a bowl of porridge and some water. For an afternoon race, you could have a couple of energy bars 3 hours or so before the off, usually while travelling to the race. During the build-up to the race sip on an energy drink.

If you are riding a long-distance event later in the day then something more filling would be needed. You could consider some pasta or possibly some red meat, such as steak, depending on your dietary requirements.

Always aim to arrive at least an hour before the race so you have time to familiarize yourself with the arrangements and it is easy to park. Seek out the organizer, sign on and obtain your race number. When changing from normal attire into race clothes, ensure you put your clothes into your race bag and

that your race bag is clearly labelled with your name, address and important telephone numbers. This is in case you have an accident and have to go to hospital, so your kit can be easily identified and ultimately be returned to you. Security is an obvious issue with valuable belongings, so take care of them.

For short-distance time trials, warm up about 50 minutes before you are due off with some easy riding that gradually ramps up to a pace a little short of race effort, held for just for a few minutes. Have an energy drink (about 750ml), and with 30 minutes to go maybe a gel. On a 25-mile time trial, if the weather is warm use a bottle. An aero bottle will not slow you down and if you drink on steady climbs, your rhythm will not be disrupted. Don't be concerned about aerodynamic penalties, as they will be minimal.

A word of warning, especially for road racing: don't race with a mobile in your back pocket. They can be damaged easily and can also injure you, with shards and so on, should you fall on this part of your anatomy. Furthermore, you won't be able to call anyone if the phone is seriously damaged. In time trials, where the chances of crashing are less, this

Beginning of a race with riders receiving instructions from the chief commissaire.

is not so much an issue and you may want to carry one for security. Many riders, unwisely, do not carry either a spare inner tube or tubular, depending on what they are running. So in the event of a puncture they could be faced with a long walk back to the HQ if they cannot call someone on their mobile and arrange to be picked up roadside.

After the Race

After the event, drink a recovery/energy drink of about 750ml and get cleaned up. If there are showers then take one. Failing a shower, rub down with a damp flannel, change, place all dirty clothing into a separate bag and put it in your kit bag. Don't pad around in bare feet, but cover them up; if taking a shower, flip-flops are a good idea.

Don't forget to hand your race number back to the organizer and collect your race licence. Pack up your belongings and load your bike into the car. You may notice that some items on the bike need attention, so make a mental note to do this upon returning home. Enjoy the ride home and reflect on the good points and not so good points – there is always room for improvements.

And as soon as you arrive home, have a snack, maybe toast or a couple of toasted bagels. Don't forget there is a very small window after exercise when your body is hungry and it will store carbohydrate more effectively than normal, so don't leave it until after showering, do it straight away.

Most of all enjoy the whole race experience and feel lucky that you can participate in a wonderful sport that many people would love to but can't.

CHAPTER 7

The Computer Age

We live in a computerized age and cycling is a sport that slots in well with computers. The focus of this chapter is an overview of the various products out there and how they can benefit your riding/training.

The humble computer, with a wire wrapped neatly around the fork-mounted transmitter and running to the receiver perched on the handlebars, has developed into a cordless version and is still very popular.

Cycle computer mounted on the handlebars.

Since the introduction of the computer, equipment has proliferated to include, in no particular order, GPS units, power meters, cadence sensors and heart monitors, to name but a few. Whilst this book will not go into too much detail on individual products it will give an overview and appraisal. There are many books on the market that deal with these products in great detail. For power meters, for example, there is no finer publication than *Training and Racing with a Power Meter*, by Hunter Allen and Andrew Coggan PhD (2010).

In addition to equipment, there is also professional software out there, such as Training Peaks WKO, which is used in conjunction with power-based products.

The majority of the riders I coach professionally all use products such as Garmin or Bryton. This chapter will explain how these products, linked to the relevant websites, can inspire your riding and provide motivation.

From a training point of view, being able to analyse your riding and compare data to previous sessions is an invaluable tool. A word of caution, though – no matter what latest piece of kit you have, you still have to get out and ride, whether on the road or indoor trainer. Keep this foremost in your mind. I've always been a results-focused coach, and a good placing, whether it is in a tough road race or quality time trial field, speaks more about the rider than the number of watts put out in training or maximum heart rate achieved. There is no point in being a good rider in the gym and then leaving it all behind on the road.

Computers

Computers basically record your speed, but the more expensive models offer many extras. The cheaper models come with a wire connecting both receiver and transmitter; a much more elegant version is the cordless type; I hate wires wrapped around frame parts attracting dirt.

Most riders connect the computer to the front wheel, which makes it redundant when using a turbo. It's much better to connect it to the rear wheel as speed can then be recorded on turbo sessions and more focused intervals can be ridden. For example, if you are riding 30-second intervals flat out, each interval can be ridden accurately to a given speed to maintain consistency.

Cadence Monitors

With a simple mounted sensor on a rear seat stay and sender mounted on the left-hand crank, this is a very effective tool to record your pedalling rpm – cadence. Many training sessions require you to pedal at certain cadences to develop efficiency, like the British Olympic pursuit squad riding at 40mph at 130rpm. Many turbo drills require cadence-based sessions and the ability to look immediately at your cadence whilst pedalling is essential.

Heart Rate Monitors

When first launched onto the market in the mid-1980s, heart rate (HR) monitors appeared to be the holy grail for training. Like most products, however, they have their limitations. Used with a recognized zone table, they can be a useful tool. They are especially useful for training on the turbo used in

Garmin cadence sensor mounted on rear stay.

Garmin heart rate monitor strap and sensor.

conjunction with a standard zone table. Even if you use a HR monitor you will still have to know how hard the effort is.

As explained in Chapter 2, the heart pumps oxygenated blood in two different ways – short, very hard efforts (anaerobic), and long, less intense efforts (aerobic). Your heart does not react quickly enough to register a reading on your HR monitor in anaerobic efforts – by the time you see a reading the effort is finished – but for slower aerobic efforts it is very useful. Taking your pulse first thing in the morning is also very useful for identifying if you have recovered from previous efforts and monitoring fatigue/illness. If your pulse is more than 10bpm faster compared to normal, this shows that something is not quite right.

Although power meters seemed to have replaced heart rate monitors as the 'must have' piece of equipment, there is still a place for HR monitors. Their simplicity of use, low cost and the insight they give into how you are performing are the key reasons that they retain their attractiveness.

There are many models on the market, but Polar is a popular make.

Power Meters

A heart rate monitor tells you how fast your heart is pumping, which is affected by many factors, such as level of hydration, air temperature, core temperature, how you slept the night before and stress levels in your life. A power meter, on the other hand, measures your true rate of work (power), measured in watts. This is similar to the horsepower (hp) quoted for a car engine.

For example, for a given heart rate, say 165, you might be showing 285W. After a period of training for a few weeks, your wattage will still show the same figure but your HR may now show 160bpm – because you have become fitter, your heart is generating the same amount of power with less effort.

Unlike heart rate, wattage is a precise figure. You will often hear track cyclists quoting wattage figures, and it is very useful being able to compare your power to weight wattage ratio with other cyclists'. To find this figure, divide your power output by your weight. For example, if you ride a 5-minute turbo test and record an average 280W and you weigh 80kg, you would divide 280 by 80 and arrive at your power profile figure of 3.5.

This figure, according to internationally recognized charts, would place you as a men's 3rd category rider. A 1st category rider would record a figure of about 6, so you can immediately see your level and the level you have to reach if you aspire to move up the rankings. The figure slightly differs for women.

Self-evidently, to improve your power/

weight ratio, you have to either lose weight or gain power. The former, in certain circumstances, can have disastrous repercussions, as instead of losing fat, you could lose muscle and in fact perform worse. A balance has to be struck.

Where it gets more complicated is in ensuring that you are comparing like with like. On what equipment did other cyclists ride? It does not necessarily follow that one cyclist riding a particular brand of equipment compared to one riding equally hard on a different one will produce the same wattage figure, even assuming both are calibrated accurately. One may be out by 10 per cent compared to the other. This is where the anomalies creep in, despite the marketing by manufacturers claiming the benefits of their system compared to their competitors'.

Another consideration is whether the pace you are riding at is sustainable. You could be riding at a constant power but your heart rate is rapidly increasing, which will result in you blowing up. Of course the reverse is also true – where the power is constant but the heart rate decreasing, indicating that you could push a little harder.

Providing your equipment is calibrated accurately then all your tests will remain the same and you will be able to see your progress or regress immediately.

All power measuring systems uses an ultra-low-power wireless transmission protocol called ANT. This technology divorces the power-measuring device from the computer head, allowing cyclists to mix and match the devices they use. For example, you could use SRM power cranks with a Garmin head unit.

Using the power data properly is key to their successful use. Like everything else, they are a tool for gaining better performance. The numbers are not everything, they have to be used in conjunction with other aspects, such as heart rate, your general condition and how you feel. You might be pushing out 300W easily but might be facing redundancy, so your overall mood may not be conducive for a good performance. You should have a clear idea on how you wish to use the equipment.

A good starting point is getting a fitness test, preferably from a nationally known laboratory – one rider I coached recommended the University of Westminster School of Life Sciences in London. You have to understand the training zones and most probably change the style of training you have completed over the years. A coach would be beneficial to advise on the data and to help in planning training sessions.

Interpreting the data needs knowledge and experience if you are to get the most out of your power meter and it doesn't just become an expensive toy that is never used properly. It is easy to become so immersed in the data that every ride becomes a statistical ritual and the sense of enjoyment from simply riding your bike is lost. Avoid 'paralysis by analysis'. If you become fixated by the numbers you also risk becoming a bore to your mates who will tire of your obsession and find reasons not to ride with you.

You will have to allocate the bike(s) that you will fit the power equipment to, bearing in mind that it's not always easy to move them once installed.

Some (not all) of the various power systems on offer are as follows.

SRM professional cranksets These are used by many professional teams and are probably the ultimate power system, with very good software and a rugged, reliable design with fully sealed bearings. The main disadvantage is the cost – over £1.5k – and that you need mechanical skills to swap from one bike to another (although this last is much easier now with single-bolt designs).

Powertap rear hubs Unlike SRM systems, these can be swapped from one bike to another (assuming you are running the same cassette configuration, for example ten-speed Shimano) and they are not as expensive as SRM cranksets, coming in at less than £1,000. However, this equipment limits your wheel choice, as you have to have the same rear wheel all the time, unless of course you run the expense of fitting out further wheels.

Polar CS/RS chainstay and derailleur
This is probably the most cost-effective set-up – less than £500 – but fiddly to adjust, and the accuracy is questionable on stationary trainers due to vibrations affecting the read-out. They can be swapped from one bike to another but the difficulty of set-up may prevent this in practice. Also, this equipment has been shown to be less than reliable with wet road conditions.

Garmin Vector pedals When these pedals came on the market in 2012, they appeared to tick all the boxes compared to the other systems mentioned above. They cost more than £1,000 so don't come cheap. With kind permission from Garmin an extract from their press release follows:

Garmin, the global leader in satellite navigation, today announced the unveiling of Vector – a high-precision pedal-based power meter – designed for cyclists, by cyclists. Vector is the lightest weight direct measurement power meter on the market, and designed for quick installation, portability, and ease-of-use. Taking only minutes to install, Vector provides accurate and reliable power data and uniquely measures and presents right and left leg power balance to ANT+™ compatible head units. Vector was announced in preparation for a world unveiling tour beginning at Australia's Ausbike, then climbing to Germany's Eurobike, and finally sprinting to Las Vegas' Interbike, where it will be prominently displayed at Garmin booths in each location.

'In developing Vector we knew we were starting to change cycling forever. Due to cost and complexity, measuring power has traditionally been the preserve of the few. Now, with Vector, the pedal-based power meter from Garmin, more cyclists and triathletes will have the opportunity to measure power more simply than ever before,' said Andrew Silver, EMEA Product Manager – Fitness. 'From picking it up at your local bike shop and installing at home in minutes, to giving you accurate and reliable total and independent leg power measurements, Vector becomes one of the most desirable solutions in the cycling market,' Silver continued. 'There's a richness in data and capabilities that come from the combination of our location of measurement – the pedals – and Vector's sensor design.'

Quick and easy: For many cycling enthusiasts, purchasing a power meter is an intimidating and potentially complicated process, often involving mechanical tradeoffs for their bikes. Vector simplifies the decisions and the process. Cyclists can now walk into their local bike shop, walk out with a Vector power meter in hand, and install it themselves in minutes. There's no need for a custom order process, no need for a mechanic, and no downtime while their bike is in the shop. With integrated cadence measurement, there are no external sensors to install, and all calibration is performed before the Vector power meter hits the store shelves. Vector's easy-to-install design makes it easy to swap between bikes, and easy to take to out-of-town events when renting or borrowing a bike. Vector's light weight and durable injected carbon fibre pedals are LOOK Keo compatible, and its ANT+ wireless pedal pod transmitters fit most major cranksets. Vector has also been designed to be easy to update as software enhancements are made, thanks to its ANT+ wireless technology. To see Vector in action, go to www.garmin.com/Vector.

Wizardry behind the watts: Vector works by

measuring the normal deflection in the pedal spindle as you pedal, throughout your entire pedal stroke. By comparing the measured deflection to a factory-calibrated deflection caused by a known load, Vector can determine how much force you're applying to the pedal. With force measurements, the cadence measurements from Vector's integrated accelerometers, and time, Vector accurately calculates watts. The force sensors are permanently and securely sealed within the pedal spindle, one of the most robust components on the bike.

Get an 'Edge' on the competition: For users already using a Garmin Edge® 800 or Edge 500 cycling computer, adding a Vector power meter will take their training to the next level. Not only will the Edge display total power, left and right leg power, and cadence, it will now also display in real time the widely adopted power metrics from TrainingPeaks™: Normalized Power (NP ™), Intensity Factor (IF ™) and Training Stress Score (TSS ™). The Edge 800 adds a new interval summary page to enhance the power-based training experience.

'Vector's easy-to-own design has the potential to make power-based training more accessible and usable by a broader range of athletes,' said Hunter Allen, founder of Peaks Coaching Group and widely regarded as a leading expert in training with a power meter. In addition, by integrating the TrainingPeaks metrics of Normalized Power, Intensity Factor and Training Stress Score directly into the Edge head units for real-time display, Garmin continues to demonstrate a strong commitment to advancing power-based cycling tools.

GPS Units

The best cycling GPS units excel in each of the following areas:

- **Features** – including climbing and descent data, calories, heart rate, cadence and power.

Garmin Vector pedal.

- **Design** – many have colour screens, long-lasting battery, water-resistant exterior and secure bike mounting kit.
- **Ease of use** – you don't want to be fiddling around whilst trying to operate the equipment as it should be an aid for your cycling and not the other way round.

There are many review sites available on the internet that go into more detail on individual models and makes. Two of the main brands are Garmin and Bryton.

Garmin seem to have cornered the market with its range of GPS units. The latest three main models are Edge 200, 500 and 800, which become increasingly complex as you go up the range, with the 800 being the top of the range.

Garmin's sports and fitness division is a fast-growing part of the company. It's obvious that significant research and development went into the 800, released in 2010 as the top model in a six-model cycling line. This is evident in its touch screen (most cycle computers are controlled with buttons), its bright display with large numerals, its never-done-before navigation features and its compatibility with power meters and other accessories.

The Garmin Edge 800 has a touch screen and can be mounted either on the stem or handlebar.

The main menu includes a 'Where To?' button allowing you to navigate by tracks, coordinates, points of interest (POIs), addresses and more.

A 'History' button gives you access to your

Garmin Edge 800.

Garmin Edge 800 displaying various information about the ride.

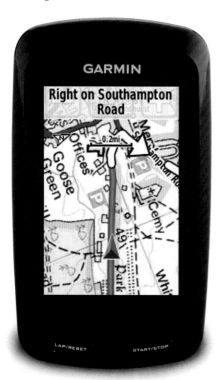

stored activities list and totals. A 'Training' button lets you set time, distance, heart rate and other alerts. A 'Virtual Partner' button lets you set up partner speed. 'Courses' lets you create and name new courses.

Data field categories include timing, distance, speed, elevation, heart rate, pedalling cadence, power, navigation, courses and workouts. There are numerous specific functions under these categories, and all can be customized to appear in your display screens.

The Edge 800 can be ordered with a wireless heart rate monitor strap and also a cadence sensor. The Edge 800 uses ANT+ wireless standard to communicate with virtually all power meters on the market. The menu system allows full integration of power stats and power range alerts.

As a user for several years of the model that preceded this one, the Edge 705, one of the most useful features is the mapping software. For example, I recently rode a sportif in Cornwall. The organizers allowed competitors to download the route, which I did firstly onto my computer and then synchronized into my Edge 705. Although the route was well signposted, I felt very confident of where I was going without the need to worry about route signs.

Mapping software is essential if you are intending to plan routes and load them into your GPS units. There are many websites offering free route planning, with GPSies.com being one of them.

Based on undoubtedly the best maps in the world, Ordnance Survey, Tracklogs is the ultimate, however. You have to purchase this software and the individual maps that cover different parts of the country, which can be expensive if you want to buy the lot. It's fine if you only want to purchase a map for your individual area.

You are able to plan routes, and the software will display the distance, total ascent and descent, maximum and minimum elevation. If using a Garmin the file saved is with a file extension .tcx.

Software Packages

Whilst operating a power meter is useful, you need to look at the data and for that a dedicated software package is essential. In this respect TrainingPeaks WKO+ has cornered the market.

WKO+

With a variety of charts and graphs, WKO+ offers Quadrant Analysis and scatter graphs, allowing users to understand both neuromuscular demands and cardiovascular improvements. WKO+ is a neutral platform so that any power meter data can be downloaded into the software.

A key feature is the Athlete's Home Page, which allows users to create and change custom charts. By doing this and by tracking fitness progression with the Mean Maximal Power Periodic Chart a rider can quickly decide whether to make changes in his or her training programme or continue with a current action plan.

Garmin Training Centre

This is much simpler package and designed for Garmin products only. Key data recorded include total distance, total time, average pace and speed, max speed, total calories, average heart rate, max heart rate, average cadence, total ascent and descent, average power and max power.

Graphs are supplied to show pace, speed, elevation, cadence, heart rate bpm, heart rate percentage and grade. There is a calendar to plan workouts and a courses section, though this is not very detailed and there is other software available such as mapping software from Tracklogs, which is Ordnance Survey digital mapping.

Whilst Garmin Training Centre is quite basic compared to WKO+ it does easily allow you to compare your rides with the drop-down menu on the right-hand side of the screen.

You may find WKO+ simply too difficult to understand and would prefer something more basic and user-friendly, in which case Garmin Training Centre may be the better choice, but be aware that you are restricted then to Garmin products.

Recording Your Training

Whatever equipment you choose you should record your training. This can be done electronically by synchronizing your recording device – Garmin, Bryton and so on – with your PC and download the data.

If you prefer something more straightforward then devise a spreadsheet and simply record the amount of hours/miles that you ride. If you want something a little more refined, showing the amount of time you spend in various zones, then an example is shown in this chapter.

Although it may not be apparent straight away, having a record of training for a few seasons is an invaluable record. When things are not going well, look back and see what you rode in a successful period and analyse this. You might see, for example, that your best form occurs mid-season when a busy period of work or domestic life is over. For some riders early season – March and April – is more productive after a good base of winter miles and a few interval sessions has pepped up their speed. In midsummer they may suffer from hay fever, which interferes badly with their riding.

Everyone is different and although you can apply basic principles to virtually everyone, how you tap into their fitness, fine tune it and turn it into results is the difficult bit. So having a diary and being to refer to it is very useful. Make filling in the diary a habitual, everyday action and it will become second nature after a period of time.

Online Tools

With the increased usage of online training websites, such as Strava and Garmin Connect to name a couple, you never need to be alone. Even though you are training on your own, you're actually not, as you are competing against someone on the Strava leader board or even against yourself, using your Garmin.

Strava

With Strava you'll need either a Garmin or the free Strava app for iPhone or Android. Strava is more basic than Garmin Connect and data are presented as a map and graph showing your speed and altitude, but it will also allow power, heart rate and cadence to be uploaded. This data can then be analysed.

Strava's fun starts when you use the leader boards to see how you match up against other riders on the same segment, whether this be a hill or certain section of road, which could even be on your way to work. A segment can be created by you by simply using the route maps. Select the start and finish line and give it a name (say King of the Mountain). Whether the segment is uphill, downhill or even flat, Strava will grade it from 4 to 1, depending on the difficulty of the climb.

When you're out for a ride, you will automatically register a time for any segment you ride through. You can also use the website to search for segments in your local area to go and target. This makes it possible to compare

Cyclo cross 2012 Training Program- December 2012

Jack Smith

	Mon	Tues	Weds	Thurs	Fri	Sat	Sun	Total training time
			Warm up 10mins with 2x30secs hard towards the end this is the same for every turbo sesson					Weekly training time in hours
AM	Commute to work and core exercises	30mins upper level 2 lower level 3 turbo ride call this Steady Teddy	Turbo, 30sec intervals, 130rpm 2min 30secs recovery, ride as many in 30mins	30mins upper level 2 lower level 3 turbo ride call this Steady Teddy	Nothing commute to work	1.5 hour Z2 ride with a couple of flat out sprints	Warm up then 10 laps of Moor Park triangle, note time. Then proceed to clubrun. Leave home just after 8am. Aim to be home before noon.	
PM	Rest	Hill workouts 4 or 5	Rest	After school cross country club.	Turbo, 10 at 10 race pace, 90-100 rpm 5min recovery			
3-Dec	Ride to work and back	Steady Teddy completed 27mins and commute. Bit of a cold on me, so no hill workouts at lunchtime	Again no turbo, still suffering from a cold.	Again no turbo, still suffering from a cold, cross country PM with School	Guests staying no training	Guests staying no training	Guests staying no training	
Time	0:15:00	0:42:00						
10-Dec	Ride to work and back	comment	comment	comment	comment	comment	comment	2:42:00
Time	0:15:00	0:00:00	0:15:00	1:00:00	0:15:00	0:15:00	0:00:00	
17-Dec	comment	comment	comment	comment	comment	comment	comment	0:15:00
Time	0	0:00:00	0:00:00	0:00:00	0:00:00	0:00:00	0:00:00	
24-Dec	comment	comment	comment	comment	comment	comment	comment	0:00:00
Time	0	0:00:00	0:00:00	0:00:00	0:00:00	0:00:00	0:00:00	
Time							Monthly hourly total	2:57:00

Summary

Recovery week same for all sessions

	Mon	Tues	Weds	Thurs	Fri	Sat	Sun	
AM	Cycle to work and core exercises	Cycle to work and back	Cycle to work and back	Cycle to work and back	Rest day Core exercises	Easy day, may ride for 90min Z2 or nothing at all	Easy day, may ride for 90min, possilble ride with Lesley on MTB's	
PM				After school cross country club	10 at 10 turbo			

Z1 108 - 116
Z2 117 - 134
Z3 135 - 147
Z4 148 - 159
Z5 160 - 168
Z6 169 - 180

Training diary.

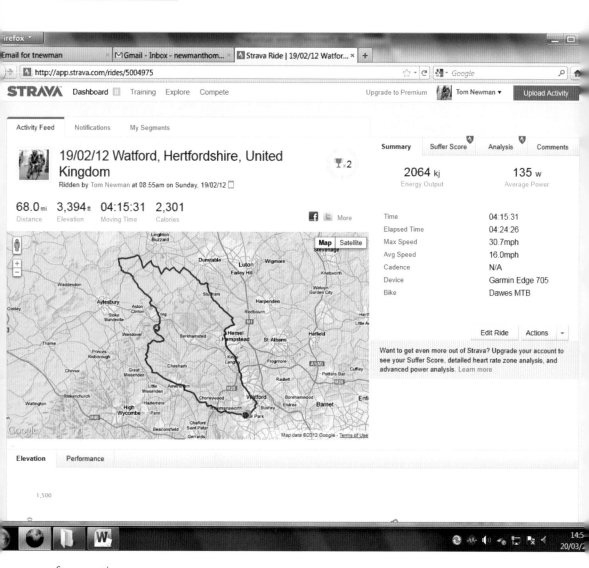

Strava graph.

your current state of fitness against, say, a local 1st-category rider on a particular climb or indeed against your club mates.

Once you have entered your athlete profile you will be able to see how far you've ridden, how many personal bests set and where you are ranked on the leader board. Every training run thus has a purpose if you wish. This can

be a useful tool, providing you record every ride you do. You can also follow other riders on Facebook and Twitter, and examine their progress – a handy way of keeping an eye on your rivals. You will also notice when your mates start staging a total onslaught on your prized KOM. Unfortunately all hope you may have out on the ride of beating rivals' times

A race-winning break with four committed riders from different clubs.

will have to wait until you are back at home and can connect to your computer to see where you are on the leader board.

Strava originated in the USA but has gained enormously in popularity, and whilst you're riding against riders in the virtual world, the participation is in the outside world. So when you are out on your ride and psyched up, you can race on a particular segment against the world. A whole new racing culture is evolving, where riders strive to get on the leader board. Many riders embrace this new kind of racing, if you can call it that, with the chance to gain prestige points based on the toughness of your ride. You also have a suffer score, based on heart rate averages.

A few cycling friends of mine were sceptical about this technology, especially having

Olleberrie Lane tucked away in the Chilterns — a Strava hill.

to obtain either a Garmin or smartphone to register their rides, but their attitudes have changed and now I regularly see their names on the leader boards.

For riders who don't belong to a club, one of the obvious benefits is to see how they measure up to local riders and have a handle on their current fitness. You can research the results of local road races and time trials online and then search for the riders' names on Strava. If they've signed up, you'll be able to see their rides and the times they achieve in training, and can compare your own. It gives you a benchmark, which was difficult to find out previously. Many people have quipped that Strava is the Facebook of cycling.

Other riders find this style of riding simply too competitive and taxing. Probably a good approach to take is only to log the rides when you feel fresh and up for the challenge, as you would not want to race every day, and not be too concerned about your ranking.

Strava can be a good training tool if used

correctly. When you want to develop your climbing, for instance, you can select certain local hills and 'go for a time' and see if you can get on the leader board. If you are a handful of seconds behind a good local rider then this can do wonders for your confidence and is something to aim for. The thing is to use it selectively.

One point some colleagues have noticed is the inaccuracies in elevation, especially if using non-Garmin GPS devices. In my area of Hertfordshire, the elevation quoted is always too low.

At a recent circuit race, I've noticed many riders recording their races with the new Garmin 800 as it is quite a sleek unit and sits nicely on the stem, downloading the information so it is viewable online. From this data, it's useful to see the speed/power necessary to compete in these events.

Garmin Connect
Garmin Connect offers a similar service to Strava in that you can upload your rides, but

Garmin Edge 800 mounted on race bike, neat and tidy.

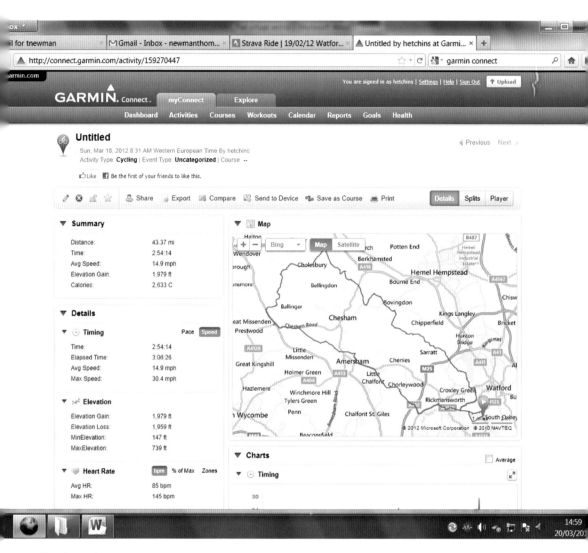

Garmin graph.

it is for use only with Garmin products. Unlike Strava, it provides a highly detailed analysis of your rides, with physical information, and creates itemized maps of your training routes.

The majority of the riders I coach use Garmins. They send me the link to their training rides so I can see how they are progressing with their training, a very useful tool. One of

the features I really like is the cadence sensor, so that high-speed drills can be monitored accurately.

Garmin will log all the information of your ride; speed, elevation, heart rate and power as well. You can choose to share this information via Twitter, Facebook or Digg or keep it private.

You can save the ride and race yourself against your previous time and monitor your progress, but Garmin Connect offers so much more than this. Its host of features include Activities, Courses, Workouts, Calendar, Reports, Goals and Health.

Whilst the mapping information is satisfactory I've found it not detailed enough. You can transform it by uploading into Tracklogs Digital Mapping software supplied by the Ordnance Survey.

Many local riders save their routes onto cyberspace, which you in turn can then save into your Garmin, very useful if new to the area. Go out and ride the routes and make variations of you own. If you do purchase Tracklogs the detail available allows you to plan route deviations very accurately. Decide on the route you want to take, look up the details in the Garmin's course section, don't forget to press the start button and off you go. All you have to do is follow the line on your Garmin for directions. When you finish, press the stop button and save the data on the unit. Upon arriving home, download onto your PC.

Nowadays one could write a book totally dedicated to computerization and talk about all these subjects in far more detail. Computerization is becoming normal now, rather than being the preserve of the elite.

Conclusion

How long it has taken to read this book depends on your appetite for knowledge and how the various examples and workouts mentioned are analysed and perhaps used to benefit your cycling.

The levels of coaching in this country have come on leaps and bounds proportionally in my opinion with our development as a major cycling nation. British Cycling's range of coaching courses have improved knowledge and there is a wealth of experience and know-how out there. Cycling as a sport gets far more coverage than it used to in national newspapers, especially the broadsheets, enticing more riders/users to join in.

It has gone a long way to dispel the old school stuff of miles, miles and even more miles. But there is a place for old-school training and its appeal for certain riders, so don't discount it out of hand.

Whilst this book should appeal to the rider up to 1st category level, hopefully those that develop into elite riders and even beyond into the professional class will have gleaned some useful tips that they take on.

Natural talent will take you a long way, but if it is not teamed with hard work, dedication and a desire to succeed then that is all it will do. There is no easy way to the top but seeking appropriate help will avoid wasting too much time with trial and error. Find a good coach – it really is worth it.

If this book helps you achieve a good race placing, clinch your club championship or ride to a personal best on an early morning time trial then it will have met its goal.

Cycling offers something to everyone, no matter what level you ride at. With age-related racing and the explosion in women's racing there is always something to focus on and aim for. The expansion of sportif (long-distance, mass-participation) events both home and abroad, which are ridden by a record number of riders, has further widened the appeal of the sport.

Whereas before the big money was spent on the golf course, these days many riders spend their hard-earned cash on bikes. It is not unusual to see exotic carbon machines lined up at the start next to the rugged and clean lines of steel frame beauties.

No matter what the bike, though, it is fitness that counts, and the rider that puts in the grimy and hard winter miles is in a better position to flourish. The camaraderie that exists amongst riders and club is very evident. I would always advocate joining a good club, dialling into the scene and tapping into the vast amount of knowledge that is available for free.

Many of us look back at our cycling careers with pleasure and fondness, remembering that unique feeling of fitness untouched before or after. The fleetness of wheel over tarmac is unrivalled when you are powering it along under your muscle power.

This book's training tips coupled with correct position, nutrition and its other features will, with time, encourage you to attain your potential, which is all you can

CONCLUSION

Age-related racing – the rider in the Henley top in his sixties mixing it with the elites, showing that age is no barrier to racing.

possibly achieve. To be a champion you have to choose your parents wisely and some will be luckier than others in their genetic heritage. But no matter, there is something for everyone.

When I first started cycling in my early teens, many of my friends who had more talent than me did not persevere with the training and fell away. Conversely, overweight individuals raised their game and achieved time trial times that were unheard of.

Some of my earlier friends have married, had children, experienced life's ups and downs, but one thing has remained paramount: the love of the sport. Frosty club runs, racing on tracks mid-week, evening time trials, riding out and back – we can look back on it all with total affection.

Continental sportif rider riding the Paris-Brest-Paris; note the lights.

Even now, out on the road there is still something to go for, whether a county sign or winning the handicap in a club time trial. With tanned legs freshly shaved and washboard stomachs honed with hours of training, the enthusiasm is still there. A new bike is always in the budget and the click of an up-to-the-minute gear mechanism whilst humming along the road is a thing of beauty.

New riders come along and we enjoy sharing our knowledge and experience with them. Embracing the latest gadgets has given the sport an extra dimension undreamt of before. There is always something coming along to keep the sport fresh and dynamic.

Get out and ride, enjoy the total experience, grab the opportunity with both hands and embrace it.

Cornish lanes – riders passing through a quiet village early Sunday morning on a sportif.

Index

RELATED TITLES FROM CROWOOD

BMX Racing

TOM JEFFRIES WITH IAN THEWLIS

ISBN 978 1 84797 454 9
144pp, 140 illustrations

Cyclosportives
A Competitor's Guide

JERRY CLARK AND STEVE JOSS

ISBN 978 1 84797 244 6
144pp, 160 illustrations

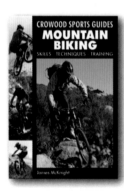

Mountain Biking
Crowood Sports Guide

JAMES MCKNIGHT

ISBN 978 1 84797 419 8
112pp, 130 illustrations

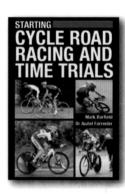

Starting Cycle Road Racing and Time Trials

MARK BARFIELD AND AURIEL FORRESTER

ISBN 978 1 84797 014 5
128pp, 80 illustrations

In case of difficulty ordering, contact the Sales Office:

The Crowood Press Ltd
Ramsbury
Wiltshire
SN8 2HR
UK

Tel: 44 (0) 1672 520320
enquiries@crowood.com
www.crowood.com